T0151700

FALSE CALM

FALSE CALM

María Sonia Cristoff

Translated from the Spanish by
Katherine Silver

**TRANSIT
BOOKS**

Published by Transit Books
2301 Telegraph Avenue, Oakland, California 94612
www.transitbooks.org

© María Sonia Cristoff, 2005
Originally published in Spanish by Editorial Seix Barral as *Falsa calma*
Translation copyright © Katherine Silver, 2018
First published in English translation by Transit Books in 2018

Excerpt from *Wind, Sand and Stars* by Antoine de Saint-Exupéry, translated from
the French by Lewis Galantiere. Copyright © 1939 by Antoine de Saint-Exupéry,
renewed 1967 by Lewis Galantiere. Reprinted by permission of Houghton Mifflin
Harcourt Publishing Company. All rights reserved.

Excerpt from *Gravity's Rainbow* by Thomas Pynchon, copyright © 1973 by Thomas
Pynchon. Used by permission of Viking Books, an imprint of Penguin Publishing
Group, a division of Penguin Random House LLC. All rights reserved.

LIBRARY OF CONGRESS CONTROL NUMBER: 2018951319

DESIGN & TYPESETTING
Justin Carder

DISTRIBUTED BY
Consortium Book Sales & Distribution
(800) 283-3572 | cbsd.com

Printed in the United States of America

9 8 7 6 5 4 3 2 1

All rights reserved. This book or any portion thereof may not be reproduced or
used in any manner whatsoever without the express written permission of the
publisher except for the use of brief quotations in a book review.

This work was published within the framework of "Sur" Translation Support
Program of the Ministry of Foreign Affairs, International Trade and Worship of
the Argentine Republic. *Obra editada en el marco del Programma "Sur" de Apoya a las
Traducciones del Ministerio de Relaciones Exteriores y Culto de la República Argentina.*

CONTENTS

FALSE CALM

For Américo C.

My father was born in the middle of Patagonia, but everybody around him spoke Bulgarian. My grandfather had avoided the kind of job in the oil industry that awaited most of his fellow immigrants by purchasing an enclave of his own along the banks of the Chubut River, in an area where the Welsh community had settled, and, on the pretext of becoming a farmer, he set himself the task of reconstructing his very own Bulgaria. With time, he managed to create a perfectly designed clone, replete with the animals, the rhythm of the harvests and the rains, the yogurt my grandmother made, the magazines written in the Cyrillic alphabet, and the Bulgarian friends who came to visit him from time to time. Whenever my father left the enclave to play soccer with friends from the neighboring farms, he knew that the rules were to kick the ball hard and speak that other language that his blond friends were speaking: from the time he was very young, he held his own in the Welsh of the playing field. Then he'd return home, where they spoke rarely or in Bulgarian. One day, when my grandparents figured he must have been about six years old, they brought him to the nearby village, Gaiman, and deposited him on a school bench. From there, by closely observing his surroundings, my father realized that most, he would almost say all, were speaking a third language. It didn't sound anything like the ones he knew, and it was called *castellano*, Spanish.

In his blind obstinacy, my grandfather had joined the project of reconstructing one's homeland in Patagonia, as so many others had attempted to do before him, from entrepreneurs such as Antoine de Tounens—who had wanted to create the Kingdom of Araucanía and Patagonia in the Andes region—to Iuliu Popper—who minted his own coins and wrote his own laws in his colony in Tierra del Fuego—to, some would say, the ancestors of the Welsh kids my father played soccer with. But my grandfather's Little Bulgaria could not defend itself against the infiltration of one of Patagonia's most distinctive characteristics: isolation. As a child, I saw this isolation as positive, as had so many European explorers in Patagonia: for them it had meant the possibility of extending their domains, for me the possibility of being in a place where routine did not hold sway. Daily schedules, meals, and scents were different there than in my daily life in the nearby city, and nobody ever asked me how I was doing in school. It was only later, as a teenager, that the isolation began to feel to me as it did to the Argentine nation-builders of the nineteenth century: as something negative. For them, it contained the threat of the unconquerable, of the territory that refused to be integrated into the fledgling nation; for me, it had turned into the very thing that was keeping me away from the country where things were happening, the people I wanted to meet, the books I wanted to read. It was a characteristic that made Patagonia a space disrupted by a kind of nightmarish logic, where I could walk and walk but still remain in the same place. Although Argentine planners had failed to carry out many of their projects for the South, they had been successful at propagating the idea that life in

Argentina passed through Buenos Aires. So, at the beginning of the eighties, I left.

I returned two decades later, when I no longer saw things one way or the other, and with time I have reached the conclusion that, as it is in my personal history, isolation is present in everything I have ever read about Patagonia. Everything, I repeat, though I don't think this is the place to make lists. I returned to write an account of this eminently Patagonian characteristic. I wanted to see the shapes it takes today; I wanted to locate it at its furthest extremes, which is why I started to look for towns that for one reason or another—not based solely on census data—could be called ghost towns. At first I picked them with scrupulous care, then I went to the places and stayed. I had at my disposal an infinite number of hours to roam around towns whose perimeters can be walked in a single hour. I sat on street corners and watched the dogs amble by. I wholly surrendered to the daze generated by the excess of light or wind or silence. There were days I felt like I was in a scene from a science fiction movie into which I had been sucked by some powerful and not wholly defined force. I saw things, many things: ghostly does not imply empty. Sitting there, almost without asking any questions or moving a muscle, without making any effort whatsoever, I turned into a kind of lightning rod, a receiving antenna. The stories came to me, the atmosphere used me as a ventriloquist. Thus arose the two-voiced narrative that follows: I was constantly trying to maintain control, but I must acknowledge that there were moments when the atmosphere spoke through me.

ONE

The photograph must be no more than five years old. Everybody in it finished primary school in the mid-sixties, so they are all between the ages of forty and fifty. There's a woman on the right with short hair and one white lock, á la Susan Sontag, who is flanked by two skinnier, more submissive-looking women. The central importance of the apocryphal Sontag is obvious, though I wonder if her authority had already been established in adolescence, or if, suddenly, on that night of the reunion, the other two had found themselves attracted to the unexpected and still incomprehensible magnetism exuded by someone they'd always felt sorry for. Most of the people who were reunited that night—according to the woman who took the picture out of a shoebox lined with fabric—hadn't seen one another for years. Almost all of them were the children of the more privileged workers in the oil industry, and as adolescents they had gone away to study or find more suitable matches. There is a row of men perched on chairs and looking straight at the camera, each with a glass in his hand. The glasses are made of plastic. The man in the middle of the row, the owner of the photograph tells me, is the one who organized the reunion. He spent about a year tracking them down one by one. Like a detective, like an avenger. He found some of them abroad: in Spain, Germany, even the United States. Quique, the man who organized everything, never moved away from here, from Cañadón Seco. And maybe that's why he got the idea; he saw that theater, which was sometimes used to show movies and other times wasn't used for anything, and he thought, why not use it as a time machine to travel back into the past. Quique is skinny, and he looks like someone who's gone through life with a small but constant malaise that he has never stopped to think about. In the photo, he's smiling at the camera, like everyone else in that row. The reunion must have taken place in the summer: most of the men are wearing lumberjack shirts. The women's attire, in contrast, shows painstaking care: each woman devoted as much thought to her dress as she did to the one for her wedding, and to the one she would have worn to the first big family funeral, if she'd had time. They look relaxed in the photo, as if they'd already gone through that inevitable moment at any class reunion when everybody is sitting around a big table and feels obliged to give an account of what they've done with their lives. Despite the evasions—the long-windedness, the innuendos, the changes of subject, the feigned deafness, the wallets opening to reveal pictures of children and/or spouses—someone would have surely admitted a failure, and most would have inferred everybody else's failures, someone would have been surprised by a revelation with sexual or economic implications, others would have been in charge of remembering those who'd died, others those who hadn't come. Everyone would have made an effort, especially that night, to show themselves off in the best possible light. Their eyes also made clear that by that point in the evening they'd already drunk a lot of the red wine that can be seen through the white plastic glasses. The photograph seems to have been taken at precisely the right moment—a labile, furtive moment—during that interval between settling accounts and saying goodbye, that swath of time that leaves room only to recall the best kind of connection that had ever existed among those present. And there, precisely at that instant of the green flash, someone had taken that photo.

It was not until later, a while later, when the owner of the photo asked for it back so she could put it away in the lined shoebox, that I saw, near the bottom, something I had previously missed, the face of someone who definitely didn't belong, someone who wasn't participating in either the reunion or the general rejoicing, who wasn't sharing hugs and whose eyes didn't look like he'd drunk too much. There he was, an impassive figure, his black hair combed back and his black eyes staring into the camera. He was at the bottom of the frame but in the middle of the scene. I stared back at him for a while, and at some point it seemed to me that all the others were, in fact, surrounding him; that he was a kind of deity in his hermitage who knew exactly what was going on while all the others, minor figures in his constellation, were waylaid by sentimentality. When I sensed that it was me rather than the lens he was staring at, I put the photograph away in the shoebox. The woman told me that was León, from the store, who had also left Cañadón after high school but had later returned.

There are two stores in Cañadón Seco. One is called *Multirrubro*, and it has a device that whistles every time a customer opens the door, the way some men whistle when they see a woman walk by. The device, however, is less sexist—the first day I went to that store, I walked in and was followed by the whistle, which sounded again exactly the same a few minutes later when two men in overalls entered—and more effective: it brings the owner out of her kitchen and everybody can buy their chewing gum, their cigarettes, their can of beer. The other store is León's, and until two years ago it was on the same block as the second restaurant in town, which has since closed, and on the same block where the town's main bar used to be, but it has also closed. To get to León's store, you have to make your way around two German shepherds lying on the sidewalk like idle Cerberuses, finally vanquished. Inside, León looks exactly as he does in the photograph: immutable, staring, his black hair combed back, surrounded by figures in his hermitage. In this case the figures are not his high school classmates but merchandise arrayed on dusty shelves: a bottle of Mary Stuart cologne, another cologne called Siete Brujas, a green melamine sugar jar whose color has faded in the sun, a plastic doll in a bag that at some point must have been transparent, two combs with pointy handles, a salt-and-pepper shaker on a fake silver tray, three jars of dried-up nail polish, a *Ludo Matic* box game, an apparatus for drying socks that turns every time the wind blows through the door. These are the remnants, what's left over from the large store his father opened in 1953, when there were as many as two or three hundred customers a day, almost all employees of YPF, the Argentine petroleum refining company created in 1922 and a crucial actor in the development of national sovereignty in Patagonia. Now, on his very best days, he barely has ten. The objects have ceased to be merely mass-produced consumer goods and have become unique items, active parts of a protective constellation in the center of which is León, who now turns to look at me, just like in the photograph.

To think, I returned for a week and stayed forever, he tells me.

He sometimes speaks, but even then he doesn't gesture or move any of his facial muscles. His right hand barely slides up to his mouth when he smokes: one quick and imperceptible motion, always the same. He makes a couple of random comments in a tone that is either sullen or reticent, at first I can't tell. After each sentence, he goes silent for a while and stares at the door. With one of these utterances he informs me that he sells tickets for the buses that travel across the northern part of Santa Cruz Province, from one end to the other, but that the buses stop only when they want to. Sometimes they're running late and then why should they stop here at all, where at most a couple of vagrants will get on. That's why he tries to stay alert, especially for the five minutes of the day when Cañadón should be a stop. It's really awful when he has to refund tickets because the bus didn't stop. Not only for the people who missed the bus but also because sometimes that's fifty percent of his sales for the day. For example, now, in about twenty minutes, one should come. I, too, look outside, and the only thing I see are the Cerberuses. He tells me that the long wooden bench that runs the length of the store is there for people who are waiting for the bus and that I can sit there even though I'm not going anywhere. I accept, and then we talk while we both look out the door, freed from having to look at each other.

• • •

To think, I returned for a week and stayed forever, he tells me.

A teenager comes in carrying a guitar in a case and sits down on the same bench as me. It's almost time, and we have to be even more alert. The three of us stare out the door. He plays in a band in Comodoro some weekends. If the bus doesn't stop, the other members of the band manage without him: there's a drummer, a bass player, and a guy who has a voice that melts your heart, so nobody complains if there's no guitar. On days the bus doesn't stop, he just goes around the corner here to some friends' house and plays the guitar for everyone as long as he's the only one who doesn't have to pay for beer. León doesn't vouch for anything the boy says, not even when he mentions the bus and its unpredictability. I'm about to ask if the dogs bark when the bus comes but something tells me that the most prudent thing to do is adhere to the policy of silence shared by León and the dogs.

There's always something terrifying, I think, about the breakdown of physical composure, which is why an epileptic attack or the private game of making faces in front of a mirror is met with so much resistance; or why it's so compelling, which is why we don't want to miss the precise moment Banner transforms into The Hulk. León exhibits aspects of such a breakdown when we see the bus appear. He rushes out from behind the counter like a cyclone, stands in the middle of the street, and waves down the driver with the same exaggerated movements used by airport runway workers signaling to pilots from far away. Then he enters the store and helps the boy load his guitar, a practical gesture that contains something maternal. When he returns, he stands again behind the counter, surrounded by his figures, his cigarette in his hand and his black hair combed back, like a dignitary from the Highlands of Peru.

To think, I returned for a week and stayed forever, he tells me.

In addition to the wooden bench and the figures on the dusty shelves, the store has a candy and snacks display. I pick out a package of cookies, as if to pay for my seat on the bench. They are crunchy, fresh. I look at the chewing gum, the chocolates: all those colorful wrappings, all intact. The candies, I suppose, are León's connection with the era he lives in, his way of being logged in to the contemporary. Of the five siblings, he's the only one who stayed in their father's store. All the others left. In fact, the sister he loves most, the one who always looked out for him, went to Spain, to Madrid. He never would have kept the store if his father hadn't objected to him studying architecture, but that's how things turned out. He agreed to pay for his studies in Córdoba on the condition that he study economics. He tried, nobody can say he didn't try, but his mind simply shut down, it refused. He was there for twenty years, in Córdoba, back and forth between trying and giving up, trying and giving up. He spent the seventies there. His father said that all the guerrillas studied architecture. He never saw any of them, in any case. Not guerrillas or friends or classmates: nobody. Only that woman he was so much in love with, who left him, just like that, from one day to the next. There was that woman and there was alcohol, more and more alcohol. And there were his attempts to study, more and more sporadic, needless to say. It was then, during that period, that his father got sick, and he came to see him for a week. After all those years living in Córdoba without ever coming back, not even for a visit, and he came. Everybody said that his father most likely wouldn't pull through, so he made the effort. His siblings, mostly his siblings, insisted on how important it was for him to see him before he died. He'd practically not talked to him at all, not in twenty years, he told them, but they reassured him that it didn't matter, not under the circumstances, that being absent at a time like that would be a heavy burden to carry around for the rest of his life. So he came for a week and stayed forever. It was really something, when he arrived, to see Cañadón after such a long time. Almost like an apparition, he'd say.

· · ·

A kid, or rather, a little boy, a chubby little boy, enters the store wearing a backpack and a school uniform, and continues walking into the kitchen. From the bench where I'm sitting I can see, through the gaps in the green plastic curtain, a Formica table, three chairs, and one of those refrigerators that has a handle like a gearshift. León follows him in. Then I hear some noises: the refrigerator door opening, water coming out of the tap, glasses or cups being placed on the table or the counter, a chair being pushed. Neither one utters a word. I start reading the biography of Malraux I have in my backpack. How can anybody, León says to me when he returns, use so many pages to tell the story of someone's life. He, his life, could be summed up in one page, even better, in one sentence. He'd actually be curious to know what the book's about, but it's been years since he's read anything. His wife, on the other hand, she reads all the time. Then he looks out the window—must be time for the supposed next bus—and I go back to my book. Why, I wonder, do I always end up choosing the heaviest book I come across in the few days before I go on a trip? Why do I have to be here, in the middle of this place about which so many people have written, reading the life of a French writer whose closest connection to Patagonia is a fleeting lover he shared with Saint-Exupéry? It's getting dark and I can barely see what I'm reading. There are electric light bulbs hanging from the ceiling of the shop, but they haven't been turned on. I close the book and see the Frenchman's black eyes drilling into me from the cover. I glance over to the counter and see that León is looking at me. By any chance, he asks me, do I know how to cure schizophrenia.

It was diagnosed years ago, León tells me. By a local doctor, from Caleta. No, he didn't get a second opinion because he doesn't need one. Whether or not waking up with anxiety in your chest that takes over and doesn't leave you alone all day long and makes you drag yourself through life is called schizophrenia, the fact is, he doesn't really care. And anyway he has no doubts about the anxiety in his chest. Nobody needs to give him a diagnosis for that. What he wants to know is how to cure it, plain and simple, how to cure it. León accompanies the question with little hops in place behind the counter, like someone who is waiting for a bus on a cold night: one of those slight movements we hope will help us recover some kind of well-being. I look at the figures on the shelves and see that they remain unperturbed. I should be able to tell him something, he repeats, there's no way I don't have something to say about it. He knew it from the start, as soon as I walked through the door that morning. That I was someone who was going to be able to give him an answer.

The boy comes back, and he says that it's already dark out and he didn't take him to padel. I figure the boy must be about eight years old, and the town gym, where he plays, is about five blocks away. The numbers don't add up. Everything depends, León tells me. Sometimes I can take him, sometimes I can't. He and his wife take turns, but apparently her work is totally unpredictable. She does the books for a metallurgy company, but it's not a steady job. They call her when they have a lot of receipts they haven't filed, paperwork they haven't finished, things that need to be organized. Twice a week: sometimes more, sometimes less. But they always tell her at the last moment, so it's difficult to plan anything in advance. The thing is that if she's not here, he can't leave the store on its own. So on those days, the boy misses padel practice, like he'll miss so many other things in life, he might as well get used to it. What choice does he have: in the end he's trading sports for an important lesson, so the boy comes out on top. León has learned from life: he learned to survive when that woman left him, he learned to quit drinking, to stay in Cañadón forever, to accept the idea that he was going to die here, even if he and the two Cerberuses are the only ones left. But he can't get used to the schizophrenia, it does him in. He can, he triumphs over it each and every morning. All that heaviness, all that bitterness. It takes all his energy, and more, just to get out of bed. Now León has turned on a little lamp, the one near the cash register, and I manage to see the same impassive face from before.

Despite the fact that the group was very united and we managed to make the best of things, something was missing; at our meetings we'd always talk about home . . . memories of the old folks, friends from childhood, girlfriends waiting for us . . . we'd get so nostalgic! . . . so sad and melancholic! But then around '47 or '48 there was a guy with a lot of guts who looked for a way to make life more tolerable in such solitude; that was Shorty Baguinay. One day he shows up and says that he's going to get married and bring his wife to come live in Cañadón Seco. Despite our friendly teasing, he did just that, he went and talked to everybody until the company gave him permission . . . He traveled to Córdoba, and returned with his wife proudly by his side . . . I don't know what the poor woman thought of these hamlets . . . but truth is, we were all a little jealous of his decision to build a future, start a family. Then it spread! . . . Puerta came next, he got married, too, and settled near Baguinay's house. The neighborhood kept growing, so they decided to give it a name. They called it Salsipuedes—get out if you can.

Memoirs of one of the first settlers in Cañadón Seco, quoted by Carlos Reinoso in his book Tiempo de crecer [Time to Grow]

The door to the store opens forcefully, the way doors open in bad movies to reveal a female character with knitted brows and blazing, imprecating eyes, except in this case the character is

different. Angélica greets me graciously and places some full
plastic bags on the ground. Those people at the office today,
they swamped her: thousands of papers, bills, problems; she
just finished. At this hour. She picks up the bags and carries
them into the kitchen. I can hear the opening and closing of
cupboard doors, the refrigerator. Based on the sounds I can
guess that the movements are swift, automatic. In between, she
shouts out: she was collecting signatures for that tuberculosis
thing again today; despite what they think, they're not going
to shut her up so fast. They're not going to come to her with
their excuses. The dignitary from the Highlands of Peru moves
the corners of his mouth into something similar to the smile
that helps more fortunate spouses listen to the other's litanies.
Angélica returns and stands halfway between the kitchen and
the store, the strips of the plastic curtain sticking to her body,
as if she were dressed for carnival or heavy sex, and she asks
me—in a way that automatically excludes the possibility of saying no—if I want to stay to eat. I look at her and think that
her parents probably had the same experience as John Huston:
they chose the name Angélica for their daughter with the hope
that she would have a direct line to the peace of the celestial
spheres, and instead found themselves with a down-to-earth
woman who knew, so to speak, the will of the flesh.

She had tuberculosis for about six months straight. And you
know how it is with those diseases: one day they're gone and
then they show up again when you least expect it. As far as
she's concerned, it's always there, lying in wait. Like herpes,
she says, you might think it's gone because the skin is smooth,
but the bug is still there, it's just dormant; always, when you're

going about your business, talking, living your life, the bug is there, dug in, well fed, a witness to each and every one of our actions. And there are thousands here just like her, all over the place. But they want to shut her up, they claim the rates have come down, that hers is an isolated case. They're the ones who are isolated, those officials, sitting in their offices, they don't see and don't want to see what's going on. She knows several neighbors who've come down with it, and they're starting an association, an organization to prevent the disease from spreading. She's written a thousand things about it. But as long as they don't admit that the disease exists, nobody will have to take responsibility for doing what should be done, that's why she's doing whatever she can. But anyway, here, where there are more dogs than people, who's going to take the trouble to think about citizens and their rights. They barely even admit that there are people. Angélica coughs—a dry, decisive cough, almost like a bark—and takes a sip of wine. León is drinking water, and his endemic muteness increases when his wife is nearby. What with everything she has to do, she also has to deal with that. This Marguerite Gautier of the year two thousand has traded sighs for curses: further proof of the curative powers of blasphemy.

Angélica reads and reads, nonstop, whenever she has any free time. She just finished *When Nietzsche Wept*, by Irvin Yalom. Fascinating, never read anything like it; it deals in depth with the subject of madness. She, she tells me, is totally fascinated by the subject. She'd lend it to me if she hadn't already lent it to a friend, that is, if she hadn't made the mistake of lending it to a friend who doesn't live here and now who knows when she'll get it back. You'd have to know what kind of house she grew up in to understand why she's drawn to madness, but that doesn't matter. She's drawn to it, and she thinks she would be independent of her family history: that's what her analyst says. And her literary workshop leader, the one in Caleta Olivia, tells her that all her stories are always so grim, why does she always return to the same subject. She recommends that she expand her horizons, think up different endings, read other things. But she doesn't see the point, what for. In the end, great writers always have their obsessions, their idées fixes. You can read or even hear—now that he appears on television—a sentence by Ernesto Sábato, and you know it's him. And why's that? Not because he repeats himself but because that's his world. And her world is the world of madness, period. Sometimes she writes about other things, but only if requested. For example, a while ago she wrote a story for a friend who lives in Cañuelas—there was a contest to describe the city and her friend wanted to enter it. She won first prize with that story. And she'd never been to Cañuelas; her friend described it to her over the phone. But that's not her real passion, she just did that as a favor for a friend. Her passion is to describe exactly what's there, beyond madness. Because it's a different world, there are different laws there. And, also, she really wants to know what we mean when we talk about madness, because there are so many kinds and such subtle differences, concepts. The number of times someone is called crazy simply because they take their time to look at things more closely, because they have a more refined sensibility than everybody else. That's what interests her, most of all: that zone where the two extremes meet, the supposedly sane and the other. Her teacher, to get her away from her subject, brought her a story by an Italian author, she doesn't remember his name right now, that has a description of a device that measures beauty. It's true, she's right about that, it's exactly what she would like to do, except with madness: have a meter that would decipher the codes, measure the levels. Because there, in that universe that everyone thinks of as deranged, there's a lot of truth. And there are some truths she still can't grasp.

TWO

The last thing he expected to find when he came back here, to Santa Cruz, was an airplane. Really, the very last. It's not that he came here to get away from airplanes, but almost. He was obsessed with them his entire childhood. There were two things he was excited about back then: the moment an airplane lifted off the ground, and the moment the priest, in the church in Córdoba, raised the host and said, *Through-Him-and-with-Him-and-in-Him-be-all-honor-and-glory-unto-Thee-O-God-Father-Almighty*. He himself never saw Christ, but he did always watch the airplanes fly past from the window of his house, which was near the Colegio Militar de Aviación. Especially at night. When everybody else went to bed, he'd stand at the window, enthralled, certain that if he went to sleep he wouldn't dream anything better. This was at the beginning of the forties, and since the thirties there'd been a school for pilots in Córdoba; whenever the priest raised the host, his eyes sparkled and he thought that it was God's will for him to be born in exactly the right place. There were even times, during those nights in Córdoba, when the roar of an airplane sounded to him like a sign from God, a coded message. He'd open the window to get a better view, even if it was winter, and he'd grab onto the iron bars his father had installed on the outside to keep out who-knows-what dangers. He'd hear the roar of the airplanes inside the bars, inside his hands. He didn't feel anything else, not the cold or his tiredness or his mother's occasional shout telling him, enough already, you have to go to school in the morning, stop this nonsense. It was on one of those nights that he clearly heard God's voice. The voice said something about airplanes, but he couldn't make it out very well. Something about faith, about destiny, about sacrifice, but he wasn't sure exactly what.

Later, years later, he made what was for him the Great Sacrifice. At fifteen, when he had to pick a specialty at technical school, he chose automobile instead of airplane mechanics. There are a lot more cars than airplanes, he told himself with a cool head, and this would guarantee he'd have steady work his whole life. You have to have integrity to do something like that: a sense of opportunity and responsibility. He's convinced of that, that not just anybody makes that kind of decision. Anybody who really understands the extent of his love for airplanes would agree with him. And that's why he always had a job here, with YPF. First in the machine shop, where he worked as a welder and blacksmith; then out in the field, with the oil pumps and the crankshafts. He retired from his job as chief of production maintenance. Been with the company his whole life. And his wife, too; she worked in administration. Until they got married, of course. Then she started taking care of the house and their child. Their children, he should say, but sometimes it slips out, he just can't say it. It's hard for him, to be honest, that whole subject. He came here when he was young, to Cañadón Seco, at the beginning of the sixties. The town was just being built, and the company was its backbone, what gave it its shape. Everybody was friends with everybody else, or at least good colleagues. That gave him strength all those nights when he didn't hear the roar of the airplanes, only the wind, when he'd ask himself why him, who'd been born in precisely the right place, why had he ended up in this wasteland. His wife, who at that point wasn't so fat or so grumpy or so bitter or so religious, helped him settle down. And, of course, his son, who was good for as long as he lasted. Those things helped him set down deep roots in this place. The pay was good, they gave him a house, health care, and the company took care of everything: they'd send in a repairman if something broke in the house, a bus for his wife if she wanted to go to the beauty salon in Caleta Olivia. It managed his life, took care of him. All of this made him feel more and more attached to the place, until he no longer had anything left from Córdoba but memories: not the accent and not any plans to return. He'd say that he wants to die here if it weren't so hard for him to talk about death.

He has to admit, though, that his day of glory was the day he found the Piper. Because, really, he had everything—a secure job, a son, a wife, coworkers, barbecues, neighbors who treated him with respect—but something, in some corner of his brain, every once in a while reminded him what he'd sacrificed. It's not that it worried him or depressed him, it simply appeared to him. Sometimes in a dream, other times when he'd be standing and staring at some spot on the meseta, which surrounds the town; out there, among the scrawny bushes, in the middle of that yellowish chalky color that wears out your eyes, a piece of metal in the shape of an airplane would appear, creating some contrast for the eyes, giving him something firm, a presence, something solid in all that desert, in all that oil. Something familiar, something of his own. Because with time he got used to this, but you've got to understand what it's like to leave that clean air, that gentle climate of Córdoba to come out here. Airplanes, for him, were the closest thing to his childhood.

Francisco insists on going bit by bit. Before death comes the discovery of the Piper. It was a summer day, he can still remember the sun shining down strongly on the tin shed that appeared right in front of them in the middle of nowhere. That sun out there, so intense, with nothing to mitigate it, forces you to squint. They'd gone to an oil field near Caleta to fix some parts on a broken pump. There were five of them. They were driving in one of those pickups the company gave them, a Chevrolet, if he remembers correctly. Someone, not him, was telling them for the third time about the fish he'd caught during his vacation in the mountains, near Esquel, when they saw, right by that road where they didn't think they'd find anything, the abandoned shed. They stopped to take a look: it seemed to be in good shape, everything closed up. They broke the padlock without much effort or many tools, and found inside, just as peaceful as can be, a '46 model Piper. A Piper PA-12. In perfect shape. The others were surprised. Francisco wasn't.

At that time, at the end of the sixties, there had been flights in Patagonia for only a short time. Aeroposta Argentina ran commercial flights, and anybody who could bought their own small plane. Air travel began to be an ally of the people of

Patagonia in their struggle against the specter of "the forgotten land." The sky was on their side. Transportation and telegraphs were the two obsessions of the first white people who settled in the South: they needed them to export, to survive, to escape. Curiously enough, today, more than thirty years later, things haven't changed very much. Moving around Patagonia is difficult, expensive, uncomfortable, erratic.

It's possible that one of his coworkers who was with him that day told his family while they were having dinner, about how that afternoon they'd come across that old shed on their way back, and maybe somebody responded. Francisco, on the other hand, didn't sleep that night. Not a wink, not for a second. The airplanes he'd seen as a child from his window in Córdoba and those he'd seen like mirages in the Patagonian desert: all of them now took the shape of the Piper PA-12 stored in an abandoned shed somewhere out in the country. He closed his eyes and saw it from afar but also from close up: the compass, the vertical speed indicator, the control panel. The airplane got assembled and disassembled in front of his eyes without him being able to do anything, neither turn away nor participate. It was as if that one image of the Piper, so peaceful, so calmly expectant, had opened the floodgates that his Great Sacrifice and his move to the South had shut, he'd thought, forever. After a while, after midnight, other images combined with the parts of the airplane: his numb hand opening slowly, etched with deep lines, after gripping the freezing bars; the physical effort his father had made to install those bars; the wheels at the moment they retract, indicating that the airplane is no longer a creature of the earth; his mother's face in the morning; the scribbles on the blackboard that grew blurry from loss of sleep. And many other things that didn't take the form of images: smells, random sentences, a sensation he had thought was lost forever. If they say that before you die your whole life passes before you in a single moment, then the Piper was that for him, like that moment before death.

The next day he arrived at the YPF garage and didn't stop talking about it. About the Piper. First he grabbed the guy he'd been working with for two days trying to fix an engine, without any luck. Then again, during lunch, when they all met up in the mess hall and ate those reheated stews, he corralled his fellow discoverers. And yes, they said, less interested in the subject than worried about their peas rolling down through the spaces between the tines of their forks. What a good idea to do something, but why, if nobody here knows how to fly. Francisco realized, almost for the first time, that it was true, he didn't know how to fly. He also thought that this had no bearing on the resurrection of the Piper. After talking to his friends, he went to people higher up at YPF. His boss told him he'd never seen him so excited. From his boss, he went to other bosses. Why not? The Piper could be the beginning of an Aeroclub in Cañadón Seco, the impetus for the development of aviation, the proof that YPF could cover all the needs of its employees in all parts of the nation. Finally, the company gave him the means—hours off and free fuel—for Francisco to set up the Flight School of Club Cañadón Seco. He designed the logo himself.

• • •

First, they hired an instructor from Pico Truncado. With him, Francisco had his first experience inside an airplane, which he'd only ever seen from the ground. It wasn't easy at the beginning. Not so much the technical issue of flying but also the reality of being part of something that he'd only ever seen from far away—desired, longed for, but from far away. The fact of being part of, immersed in, what he'd only seen from the outside, made him feel uncomfortable, strange. Sometimes, it even became physical: he'd look at his hands before taking hold of the stick and see them as foreign objects with their own lives, beings that would act independently of him, and who knows where they'd take him. It's not easy to start doing something you've watched so much, much less that you've longed for so much. If he'd had access to an airplane before, when he was young, that wouldn't have happened, he was certain. But he'd only ever managed to get inside airplane engines. There, among those spark plugs and belts, he'd glimpsed the truth of flight, the core that made those machines shoot through the air like arrows from heaven. That's as far as he'd made it, but flying inside, never. Making that transition wasn't easy. And it disappointed him—he had to admit it. Those powerful visions that plowed through the sky like ghostly apparitions entailed, from up close, from inside, a series of synchronized commands, a compass, ground communications, technical checks. Control, a lot of control. The certainty that he could never allow himself to get carried away by any sensation, that he had to always maintain control over everything. As a child, there in Córdoba, he'd associated flying with the fantasy of losing himself, of happily giving himself over to the forces that govern the world. Now, sitting in front of the control panel, more than three thousand feet in the air, there wasn't the slightest possibility of doing anything like that. Flying, it seemed to him, would condemn him to permanent vigilance, to a state of high alert, which had to prevail over everything else. The instructor from Truncado would sit behind him, and he'd start to talk to him and wouldn't stop; he was constantly giving him instructions. Francisco had to make sure that everything was adjusted so that the rate of climb would be correct, and he couldn't look at anything ahead of him or below him. There were so many things he had to pay attention to all at the same time. The altimeter, the speedometer. And all the possible dangers: what to do if the airplane suddenly lost altitude, how to make an emergency landing, how to react to an engine problem. Data, quick reflexes, response capability: you had to hold onto all of that, hold it in reserve. One afternoon, sitting in that small cockpit, waiting for the pilot to arrive, he asked himself if he'd made a mistake: if just looking at airplanes wasn't what he really liked to do.

All that changed the following year, 1972, when the other instructor arrived. With him, he discovered how far he could go with flying. With him, he began to use his skills to carry out certain technical maneuvers: make a tight turn, a 360-degree turn along the flight line, an emergency landing. With him, he learned how to turn it all into a game, because in the end, what else was it? It might be dangerous, he admits, but that's no reason for it not to be a game. That's what he felt while he was flying, total serenity, and suddenly he felt a drop, a five-hundred-foot descent in one minute; he felt like he was playing hide-and-seek, like in Córdoba. This instructor, his name was

Pablo, barely ever talked to him about technical issues. And that's after Francisco had told Pablo when he first arrived that he should watch him closely, that even though he knew more about flying than anybody else in the whole area, that didn't mean anything, he'd soon see that it was the typical case of a one-eyed man in a country of the blind. Pablo told him that he had a sister who was blind, that he shouldn't talk like that. And not a lot more. Later, in general, he refused to talk about flying. Francisco can't say how he learned so much from him. Maybe it's not about talking. That must be it. He'd say things, but they'd be random things, nothing very explicit, nothing like the barrage of instructions he'd gotten used to. For example, he'd say, the compass. And then Francisco would realize that they were lost, that they'd taken off with the intention of going north, toward the meseta in Chubut Province, but there was the sea beneath them. The ocean, the Atlantic, that is. The first few times, Francisco would comment on what was going on, announce what he was going to do, even what he was doing. He'd say, for instance, there's the ocean, so I should turn northeast, that now I realized there was no wind resistance; but the other one, nothing. Silence. A silence that made him feel disoriented, childish, redundant. And it left him totally on his own. How was he supposed to make the turn to the northeast? A quick tight turn, or a large open one? And should they really go northeast? I can't read the instruments, he'd say at other times, as if to raise the alarm, provoke some kind of response, but Pablo wouldn't answer. There were times up there when he felt like letting go of the controls and grabbing him by the neck to force him to react. But he always had to shake off his anger as quickly as possible and react himself, act before it was too late. With time, however, he realized that those few words were all he needed, that deep down he knew that Pablo was there and that if, through his own fault, Francisco's fault, they came within a few meters of the ground, Pablo would know how to take control of the plane. He knew how to calculate the last minute he could react, the very last minute, the one that made the difference between continuity and catastrophe.

When he did talk was in the mornings, when he would stop by his house to pick him up. Early, at dawn. He, Francisco, would have just put the water on the stove and then he'd hear Pablo's greeting, which was always the same: a few knocks on the wood shutters that to Francisco sounded like the scratching of a cat who'd inadvertently remained outside on a cold night. It always sounded the same, even if it was summer and it wasn't cold. He'd let him in and they'd sit down at the kitchen table to drink maté. Everybody else in the house would be sleeping—at that time "everybody" meant his wife and his son. His other son, not the two who live with him now. So he and Pablo spoke quietly, in a whisper. Like that, everything sounded like a secret. That's when Pablo told him about his first flights, about the woman he loved who wrote him letters from there, from El Palomar. Francisco never met her, but he imagined her as affectionate and stern, pretty, a good mother. Even though she couldn't have been a mother because they didn't have kids, he imagined she had that maternal quality. He imagined her as one of those women you could live with in peace. The kind of woman every pilot needs. For the nerves. You've already got whatever's going on up there, alone, confronting the forces of nature. He imagined all that based only on what Pablo told him, even though he didn't say much about what she was like. He talked, instead, about the things she did. But there, they never talked about flying. Once Francisco tried to ask for an explanation about something, some advice. What to do if there's a stall, for example. We'll see when we're there, Pablo would tell him, and he'd continue his story, say something else. Francisco would leave the burners on at that time in the morning, always, in winter and summer, to warm up the kitchen, and still today, when he remembers those conversations, he hears them with the sound of the burners in the background: that dull hissing sound, like gasping for breath through constricted airways.

That stuff about Pablo's ability to recognize the exact moment before a catastrophe, it's not just a manner of speaking; it's something he himself witnessed, with his own eyes. He still remembers that day. It was May, after they'd been flying together, after he'd been training with Pablo for more than six months. Nothing out of the ordinary had happened until that minute, or rather until a few minutes before that one. The scratch, the dawn chat, the maté, the secrets around the table, and a few words in the Piper. Francisco doesn't know what happened, not even today does he have an explanation for it. But something, some kind of mysterious ray got in the way of his skill and prevented him from landing. As simple as that. He was there sitting in front of the panel—not for the first or the second or the tenth time, it was something he thought he had under control—when suddenly something stopped him, blinded him. Something that prevented him from landing, descending, touching ground. A kind of blackout that made his hands unable to react, his brain unable to make decisions. A kind of malignant murmur, which sedated him, hypnotized him, and rendered him lifeless. Like a paralyzing gas, emitted not from the enemy camp but from his own person. The altimeter showed that they were at an altitude of two thousand meters, he'd already sent the signal by radio, but everything else was on hold. He couldn't think of the descent. It happened to him many other times over the years, after that, something vaguely similar, he thinks, trying to find an explanation. Something that doesn't totally paralyze him but makes him resist the descent, as if deep down he knew that the moment the airplane wheels touch the asphalt of the runway marks the reencounter with a whole series of commitments, agreements, and relationships that he doesn't quite understand, not when or how they were made. Or why. There, during those final moments before landing, it seems like none of those things have anything to do with him. As if he were in one of those movies they show on Sunday afternoons, where somebody wakes up having taken on somebody else's life because they gave him a bad blood transfusion or mistakenly operated on his brain. Descending is, at those moments, like queuing up at the window of daily life. Intolerable, even unfair, he'd say.

The thing is that on the day he started telling me about, all that denial reached such an extreme, such a high level of tension that, instead of exploding, it paralyzed him. He exploded, but inside, it was a kind of internal stampede that raced through his veins until it stopped his circulation, dried up his brain; a backfiring, he'd say. By the time he came to, Pablo had taken command of the Piper and was preparing to touch down.

Francisco thinks he said something, mumbled some disjointed words to himself or to the mystery that can dwell in the most unexpected places. He doesn't remember that part very well, only the physical sensation of returning home. A feeling of exhaustion, he'd call it, if by exhaustion we mean feeling like an amorphous blob that some mighty force is dragging through the streets. Defeat in every cell, but not like the counterpart to some success; an existential defeat, the curse of having been born. That afternoon he didn't go to work at the garage; he went straight to bed and stayed there, like a corpse. Every time Pablo's face appeared there on the white ceiling, a wave of shame, or maybe even humiliation, crashed through his body. He tried to go over in his mind where the mistake had been made, but the chain of events would break; the engine pressure, the oil temperature . . . and he wouldn't be able to go any further because the wave would crash and he wouldn't be able to think anymore. Why precisely now, when he'd overcome so many fears, passed so many tests, when the airplane offered barely any resistance, when they'd achieved a communion in which neither one gave instructions to the other but instead glided, united, through the sky together. Never before, not even the first few times, back when even the control panel looked like hieroglyphics, had Pablo had to take over. He'd always managed, even precariously, to work things out. How could this have happened to him now? All his life he'd always carried on: he'd just finished mastering engines with lateral valves and already he was dealing with fuel injection engines. Everything built on everything else, he learned one thing and that made him able to deal with the next. Why couldn't it also be that way with the airplane, with flight?

It was, he thinks, already dark out, when his wife lay down on the old mattress, and for the first time in his life it occurred to him to attribute it to divine punishment. His greed had blinded him and paralysis had been the way life had reminded him that he had betrayed the Great Sacrifice, that he had forgotten his wise renunciation. It's admirable how there's something in us that helps us be coherent, even in our moments of greatest distress. What this confirmed for him was that he was made to look at airplanes, not fly them. He'd even considered talking to his wife, trying to explain his paralysis, his punishment. Ask her if it had ever happened to her. His wife was snoring, next to his ear, like she did every night, and he thought it better not to wake her. The truth is, or so he's come to think over the years, there are things couples shouldn't talk about. Like Gustavito, for example. Because all he'd ever wanted was for his son not to have the conflicts he'd had; if he liked airplanes, he wouldn't be against it, he wanted him to learn about them, be around them from early on. That's why as soon as he started walking, Gustavito was always hanging out with him at the hangars, around the engines. You could say he grew up there. The kid loved airplanes as soon as he saw them, all on his own, it's not like his father talked him into it or anything. How could he guess that later, when he was twenty-three, he'd crash in one. In the very same Piper that Francisco had rescued that afternoon from the metal shed with the sun reflecting off it. That's what his wife didn't understand and never would: that he couldn't have guessed it that afternoon.

• • •

In November 1929, before the end of the first of the fifteen months he lived in Argentina, Antoine de Saint-Exupéry flew the inaugural flight of Aeroposta Argentina to the South. He, like Francisco, knew airplanes as well as he knew engines; at the end of the First World War he'd been recruited into the air force, but since he still had a lot to learn, he, too, started in the maintenance division, as a mechanic. By the time he arrived in Argentina, he'd already lived the life of a quasi-legionnaire at an outpost in the Sahara, where he was sent by the company. His flights in Patagonia left him deeply impressed by two things: the longing with which people awaited the arrival of airmail, and the night. He writes about the latter in *Night Flight*, which appears to be a novel-memoir about those flights that Jean Mermoz thought up to save the company from bankruptcy, though it is really a book about the night. About the dangers of flying, and above all about his inability to recount it, the difficulty of turning experience into a story.

> The sky was blue. Pure blue. Too pure. A hard blue sky that shone over the scraped and barren world while the fleshless vertebrae of the mountain chain flashed in the sunlight. Not a cloud. The blue sky glittered like a new-honed knife. I felt in advance the vague distaste that accompanies the prospect of physical exertion. The purity of the sky upset me. Give me a good black storm in which the enemy is plainly visible. I can measure its extent and prepare myself for its attack. I can get my hands on my adversary. But when you are flying very high in clear weather the shock of a blue storm is as disturbing as if something collapsed that had been holding

up your ship in the air. It is the only time when a pilot feels that there is a gulf beneath his ship.

Another thing bothered me. I could see on a level with the mountain peaks not a haze, not a mist, not a sandy fog, but a sort of ash-colored streamer in the sky . . . I tightened my leather harness as far as it would go and I steered the ship with one hand while the other I hung on to the longéron that ran alongside my seat. I was still flying in remarkably calm air.

Very soon came a slight tremor. As every pilot knows, there are secret little quiverings that foretell your real storm. No rolling, no pitching. No swing to speak of. The flight continues horizontal and rectilinear. But you have felt a warning drum on the wings of your plane, little intermittent rappings scarcely audible and infinitely brief, little cracklings from time to time as if there were traces of gunpowder in the air.

And then everything round me blew up.

Concerning the next couple of minutes I have nothing to say. All that I can find in my memory is a few rudimentary notions, fragments of thoughts, direct observations. I cannot compose them into a dramatic recital because there was no drama . . .

. . . I landed near by and we were a whole hour getting the plane into the hangar. I climbed out of the cockpit and walked off. There was nothing to say. I was very sleepy. I kept moving my fingers, but they stayed numb. I could not collect my thoughts enough to decide whether or not I had been afraid. Had I been afraid? I couldn't say. I had witnessed a strange sight.

What strange sight? I couldn't say. The sky was blue
and the sea was white.

Wind, Sand and Stars, *by Antoine de Saint-Exupéry, translated by*
Lewis Galantière.

That morning, Francisco rose from bed like an automaton; his
wife was still snoring. He got up at dawn, out of sheer force of
habit, like he used to when he first started to fly and then later
when he worked in the shop. He could have stayed in bed a
little longer, taken advantage of his new life with no scheduled
flights, an empty, aimless life. He brewed some maté, but this
time he didn't leave the burners on. His body was numb—no
amount of heat could fix it. The house beyond the kitchen felt
like a huge empty space, like the ravenous mouth of a giant
waiting for him to fall into its jaws. How difficult it was for him
to do alone what he'd always done accompanied. Now what
would he do, for example, when he ran into Pablo in the street,
or at the mess hall, or when Pablo would bring them airplane
parts to fix in the company garage. He speculated about all
of that while he sat there at that cold table. For a moment he
thought he heard a scratching on the shutter, but he quickly
dismissed the idea. The mind can betray us, as he well knew.
Then came the knocks, and when he opened the shutters he
saw Pablo, his face the same as every morning, saying that it
was a little late but they should leave now. That today seemed
like the ideal day for Francisco to go alone.

In his book, *Take-Off,* Daniele Del Giudice describes something
similar. He says that the day after having flown his worst flight,
when he was on the verge of crashing into the middle of the

ocean because he'd forgotten to do something, like lowering the lever for the flaps for takeoff or some other mistake that for a pilot is pathetic, inconceivable, that was the day his instructor told him that it was time for him to make his first solo flight. When he, in shock, asked him why today, his instructor told him, summarily: "Because of your mistake. Thanks to the mistake, you were able to see the mistake."

That day, Francisco took off alone and landed perfectly, as if touched by magic. Not a single hesitation, no sign of instability, doubt. He felt neither fearful nor triumphant, and had only the sense that he'd nailed it. Up there, alone, he felt for the first time that something had become whole, that he was where he was supposed to be. That it had been very exciting to watch airplanes through the window, but there was no comparison, this was on an entirely different scale. His old admiration for airplanes seemed ridiculous. A mere sporting event, no matter how much he'd thought he was in touch with the divine. He didn't think about anything or anybody. Not even Pablo, who was carefully watching everything from the Aeroclub. He manipulated the levers as if each were a microworld unto itself. The compass, the altimeter, they all seemed like partial representations of an infinite system that was revealing its secrets to him for the first time. Those numbers and those directions ceased to be merely facts: they were part of a code that allowed him, for the first time, to be immersed in a situation in which he neither expected nor needed anything else. Up there, when he's in control, nothing is fixed in relation to anything else, not even in relation to the landscape waiting passively there below. The meseta's furious whiteness, which has effectively hypnotized so many. It's a state of total suspension, literally. And then the landing: perfect. A poem. It almost left him with no time to think about what was waiting below. The heaviness of the contact with the ground was lighter, deferred, not part of the flight at all.

Francisco is telling me about his first solo flight while he sands the propeller of a model airplane. The light enters from the east into the shop that was built in his backyard a few years ago, when he retired from YPF. He traded one shop for another. Where could he return to, otherwise? Because at some point, you always have to descend from the airplane. Home, with Latin American telenovelas on TV? Home, among the crocheted tablecloths his wife never stops making, as if she were a spider? Home, with those two hooligans, who do nothing, who must be around twenty years old and still haven't finished school? They're good kids, but you can't expect much from them. Not like Gustavo; all you had to do was look in his eyes when he'd enter the hangars: a person interested in something, enthusiastic. There's not a chance with these two. He and his wife have done everything possible, but, also, you've got to see how things were from the get-go in order to see where they can possibly go. The two boys—he should say his sons, his wife tells him that all the time, he'll do it soon—are the sons of a prostitute who worked in Caleta. Who knows what the poor kids suffered before they adopted them. The things they've seen, the suffering. Because childhood is so important, it's not like you're just little and in any case you don't understand anything, and afterwards you don't remember anything. His thing with airplanes, for example. When he used to watch them from his bedroom window in Córdoba. Everything still comes back to him—all he has to do is close his eyes—as clear as day. They adopted them when the older one was five and the younger one three. They're brothers. Same mother, that is, because nobody ever knew about the fathers. Then the mother died. Murdered. Nobody knows how or who. And it was all pretty hard on him and his wife at first. Especially because of the neighbors, who didn't always react as they would have liked. Weird, to tell the truth. People you thought of as your friends for years, and then suddenly they don't say hello because you've adopted the children of a prostitute. That's because this town started rotting about twenty years ago. Before, when everybody was like one big family, that wouldn't have happened.

It must have been because of all these things that his wife sought refuge in the church. Not him, that's why he has his shop. It took him years to understand that when someone doesn't understand, doesn't share, it's better not to insist, better for each to go his own way. Like for example, what happened with the airplanes in the seventies, when YPF was still YPF, and he managed to make the company invest, support him, establish the Aeroclub, which in the end was good for everybody. Even for the company, because after a while, once he'd mastered it, he started making flights that YPF paid him for, because they were useful. He'd fly to Catriel to bring equipment, to Río Gallegos to bring food when a crew got stranded in the snow. Then, when this whole mess started, ciao. There was no way. Everybody was grabbing what they could, every man for himself kind of thing that nobody could have predicted during those years when everybody was on the same page. Now, there's nothing left: not the Aeroclub, not anything. Nothing we can all do as a group. Except go to Mass. Things look better from here, with the engines. This shop is his daily escape, his last flight.

There's a large wooden table covered with boxes of nails, bolts, and screws. Scattered around elsewhere are parts of engines, spark plugs, clamps. And in the air that rancid odor of greasy tools, tools being used. Many of them are hanging on a wooden wall panel, and there are signs with aphorisms posted around the room: "Strong souls reject lasciviousness as sailors avoid the shallows," one says. There are no chairs, just some wooden stools, very high with very narrow seats, so that nobody even considers settling in or overstaying their welcome. "Failure starts when effort stops," says another. From the ceiling hang at least ten model airplanes of different kinds: a SuperStar 40, a Picurú, a Piper Cherokee, a Piper PA11. Francisco assembled all of them. Been doing it for years now. It's taken him a long time to complete them all, and he does it only at special moments. In the end, it doesn't do anybody any good. He assembles them just to hang them up, so they keep him company. Once he gave one to a friend, but one day he went to visit him and saw that his son had smashed it and thrown it in with his other toys in the backyard. As if that's where it belonged, with the toys. Francisco talks, less concerned about looking at me than wedging in a couple of pieces that don't seem to want to fit into the engine he's assembling. Anybody taking a quick glance would think that he was talking to himself. Through the open window blows a gentle breeze, and the light outside is fading. At this time of day, from my stool, I can no longer see his features. I see him more as a black silhouette in a mechanical battle, surrounded by airplanes that spin around his head as if they were birds of prey.

THREE

Ramiro holds out the package of assorted biscuits he's been eating constantly, a sign that I should take one if I want, and when I accept, I confirm what I feared: there are no chocolate ones left and the one I choose tastes of damp. We're sitting on the stairs of what used to be the town's theater, kitty-corner from the church. Here, in Cañadón Seco, the diocesan clergy has a seminary where aspiring priests spend their first year of training. They take classes in Latin and introduction to the liturgy, they learn to cook and pray, and they begin to grow accustomed to what it means to live in a cloistered community. A watershed year: those who survive continue their studies in Buenos Aires, at the seminary in Villa Devoto. No, Ramiro's never been to Buenos Aires. Never even been to Bahía Blanca. But the truth is, he doesn't care. He has no interest in going to any city, and he's already thinking that when he finally takes orders he's going to ask to be sent to some town in the middle of nowhere, like this one. He doesn't want to be a priest just to stick the host into the painted mouths of ladies wearing perfume and fur stoles. He might have his doubts, but that's one thing he's sure of. The way his mother reacted when he told her—and till then she'd been the only one who supported his becoming a priest. Because his two sisters never spoke to him again after he made the announcement at home, about two months before coming here. And his girlfriend, well, his girlfriend told him that this year she was going to wait for him to see which love was stronger. All very romantic, but he's sure she's been partying these last few months. He'll find out soon, when he goes home. It's July now, exactly one week before they have a month vacation. Those who drop out this first year don't wait till December: they simply don't return from this vacation, the priest who runs the seminary told me this morning.

Until now he's been handling it well, Ramiro continues; must be about three days ago, not more, he began to feel this nausea, a kind of burning in the pit of his stomach that rises and presses on his chest. Especially right after he wakes up: that's when he feels it the most. And there's no thought or prayer that works. It will go away, he figures. He hasn't told anybody here, in the seminary, because they all have enough of their own problems and also because he's had it for only a few days, for sure it's something temporary. And obviously his girlfriend will get an earful if he finds out that she's been partying: the year ends in December and a deal's a deal. Anyway, he's prepared for the worst, knowing how women are. And maybe it'll even be for the best to find out the worst: not that she's gone out with a bunch of guys while he's been here, spending his nights alone in his narrow bed. Better to find out that she went out with only one and that one happens to be his best friend. Or something of that nature. Something that would make it easier for him to come back here for good. Give himself wholly to God, without regrets or doubts. Slam the door on what came before and stop feeling pulled between one thing and the other.

. . .

At the seminary there's a room that fulfills the function of, we could say, a library; it has two computers and some wooden bookshelves buckling under the weight of rows of books, an eclectic collection that seems to be the result of meager and haphazard donations rather than any plan for organized study. On one of those shelves Ramiro found the book that helped him the most during those first six months. More than any advice from the Father or Bible readings or the group prayer sessions they hold several times a day. He puts the package of biscuits down on the stairs, opens his backpack, and shows me the tattered volume: a biography of Charles de Foucauld. At twenty, the same age Ramiro is now, De Foucauld was the unruly son of a French aristocratic family that no longer knew what to do to make him stop squandering the family fortune and to separate him from his unsuitable girlfriend. Later, though not that much later, he joined the army and fell in love with the Arab world. A feeling that was not, as it turns out, unique at all among European soldiers who arrived as colonizers in Africa or Asia, except that De Foucauld, with his passion for extremes, took his love to several of them. Before turning thirty, when the army had already expelled him for immoral conduct, he dressed up as a rabbi and spent a year exploring Morocco, and returned with geographic information useful to French military strategists. That journey proved crucial. The panic he felt for the day and a half that he spent as a hostage in the Moulouya River valley and the constant threat his excellent disguise as a Jew subjected him to in the Arab world, revealed to him the path he had sought for so long. At that particular extreme, facing constant danger, he felt close, even akin, to Jesus. "Until he died, he would keep the memory, the obsession, even the desire to know that his life was being threatened," says a different biographer from the one Ramiro is reading. So he decides to completely remove himself from the privilege that his social position made him take for granted and plunge headlong into the lower spheres, specifically desert tribes. He would spread throughout that terra incognita the message he had found so difficult to concoct. He would wander around, carrying that message like a priceless quarry, as if it were the essential cipher that was imperative to deliver to the other side of a mined field. I read the first pages of the book that Ramiro pushes on me, as he did the package of biscuits, and I find obsequious prose, weighed down by adjectives. It's from there, Ramiro says, from him, that he derives his strength. Mostly, the part about preaching in the desert. But this week not even De Foucauld can rid him of his nausea; it's like a fire that starts in his stomach, rises up into his trachea, then dies down when it gets to his throat. Right there, when it reaches the threshold where he's about to be rid of it, it refuses to turn into vomit or a sentence. It's nothing. I figure Ramiro will manage to hide the book among his things and take it home with him.

The altar table offered an encounter with God, the seminary table, with communal life, I was told by the seminarian who invited me to have lunch with the group. I wondered if it might be too much for me, but his appeals won the day. He's in Cañadón giving classes and helping the director; these are his last duties before he takes orders. This place—they thought it out well—has everything needed to serve as a test by fire at the riskiest stage. A high percentage of the aspiring seminarians at the table are in their early thirties, contrary to what I expected. They are the ones who avoid me the most. There's one who looks like he was plucked out of *The Celebration* or some other movie from Dogme 95: tall, blond, and with traces of some subterranean sorrow in his features. He doesn't offer me even a minimum of verbal civility, something quite difficult to carry out at a table of fewer than twenty diners and where the imperative to be sociable holds sway. He has an excuse for not paying any attention to me: he's in charge of cooking and serving the food. Those sitting closest to me are all Ramiro's age. One of them, wearing a Boca jersey a few sizes too large, explains in great detail the problem that had him stuck on the computer all morning, as if asking for a solution, and everybody looks at him in the same kind of daze as I do. The meat we are eating was donated by somebody who owns land nearby, and the warm orange Tang we are drinking is, I assume, another of the tests by fire the seminarians of Cañadón Seco must undergo. At a certain point, I look to my left, and my eyes meet those of the apocryphal actor as he quickly and warily turns away. I figure that when someone at that age decides to make a go for an ecclesiastical career, they've already swallowed more than one bitter draught. I also figure that he believes I am capable of intuiting those draughts, which is true, though I would never be able to differentiate them from the ones imbibed by somebody not aspiring to the priesthood. A series of frustrated efforts, the sensation of being inadequate, the need to escape everything, anxiety, rage at always making an effort, at humiliation, at meaninglessness. I'm worried that at some point, as in

The Celebration, the blond man will bang his fork against a glass, stand up, and start talking.

Ramiro eats biscuits after lunch, as well. He's been told that there are still followers of Father De Foucauld, but he needs to find out a little more. It seems they live in partial hiding, dedicated to spreading the word of God, but not from the pulpit or anything of the sort. They live in slums, on cargo ships, in underground mines, in places where nobody comes to talk about God or anything else. But they don't talk about God, either: they simply live like everybody else there, like another miner, another sailor. It's not about spreading the message with words but rather through example and silence. Honestly, he doesn't know, he doesn't know if he'd be able to do it, but sometimes, when he's seized by doubt, that extreme really attracts him, gives him strength. He doesn't really know why. And he's never told anybody before now; if he ever told his mother, the poor thing would die; at least now she finds comfort in the thought of him walking around town in his black cassock, like one of those movie actors who always plays handsome priests, and everybody goes to see them and greatly respects them, and they will all congratulate her on the wonderful son she has. Maybe, if that happens, even his sisters will speak to him again. Though for sure the girls will get over it sooner, probably even by now, next week, they've both already invited him to come to their houses to eat, to do something with their kids. He has two nieces and a nephew. But they don't call him uncle because he'd kill them; Ra-mi-ro-is-my-name, he tells them every time they start with the uncle crap. His father? His father doesn't care, he thinks. As long as he doesn't do drugs or get into debt, everything's okay, he can do whatever he wants. His father was never very communicative. When he was little, his mother would make all of them stay awake, he and his two sisters, to wait for their father to come home so they could eat together. As a family, she'd say. But what for? He'd arrive, sit down, and remain silent for the whole meal. He'd barely say, oh, really? when they'd talk about something that happened at school or in the neighborhood. Not a peep from the guy. It must have been because of the job he had, honestly, many people wouldn't feel like saying much, or maybe he thought it wasn't good for his children's upbringing to hear about the prison and the prisoners and the wardens. One night, he remembers, his father came home from the prison all beat up. Apparently a prisoner tried to escape when he was on duty, but when they ran after him one of his own colleagues grabbed him, another prison guard like himself, and gave him a blow that he's only now recovered from. That night his mother canceled the dinner that she'd always considered a sacred ceremony, gave them something quick to eat, and locked herself up in the bedroom with their father. The three of them pressed their ears against the door and managed to hear what had happened, more or less, but they weren't really sure because his father was sobbing between sentences. For the first and only time in his life, he was crying like a baby. That's why none of the three felt like asking him about it the following day.

FOUR

The stray dogs that swarm around Cañadón Seco are helping me perceive with much greater clarity what under other
circumstances appears to be much more ambiguous: the precise moment a spell breaks. Or, whatever we call that moment
when a place feels compelled to expel an intruder, who in this
case turns out to be me. This tends to happen to every writer
in pursuit of a story, who at first is welcomed by a place—its
people, its institutions, its landscape, and, as I am finding out
now, also its animals—with open arms, eager to find out what
she's researching, what she needs, how they can help. During
that initial period, the most insignificant question—what time
is it, for example –might lead to a story about the clock that
used to be in the main plaza during the 1920s and then was
destroyed by a storm at the beginning of the thirties, followed
by the story of the struggle between this alderman and that
alderman about who can claim credit for installing the new
clock that's there now. The mere mumblings of a stranger can
produce an excess of verbosity that one must know how—be
able—to translate into the language of hospitality. This on-
slaught of information creates a special kind of solitude, which
is unique, different from all others. One effect of that solitude,

which I've sometimes experienced on a particularly tired night, is to consider sharing a personal story of my own, talk about a problem that I know I will have to deal with when I return home—for example, that I expect a meeting of the residents of my building to discuss for the third time what we should do about the pigeons that have settled into the eaves and don't let anybody get any sleep—and that's when I've noticed a mild shock, an expression of perplexity, as if they'd glimpsed, through the crack in the door left ajar, the newly arrived guest as she is undressing to get into bed.

But there always comes that moment, as I was saying, when the spell breaks, when the locals' eagerness to tell their stories, so abundant at the beginning, starts to wane. Like in love, when the end is presaged by a lack of excitement in shared stories—and not in shared sex, as psychologists so often assert on television. For a writer, it's not always easy to determine the precise moment when the boundaries surrounding a place, which define it, begin to shut her out—like the tissue that produces pus as a barrier against a foreign object—and finally expel her. By the time a series of much more subtle and contradictory signals renders that moment recognizable, it's already too late. It's easy to get confused, and then the trap is set: the one investigating goes from being the observer to the observed. The fabric is turned inside out, like the reversible parka of my childhood, and the place scrutinizes her, she becomes the one under the spotlight. At that point she must flee, run off and hide, as if she belonged to a species that cannot be exposed to a certain kind of light.

In Cañadón Seco, the dogs let me know precisely when that moment arrived. They were clear and precise, leaving no room for ambiguities. By then I'd already been in town for a while. I'd walked around the entire place an infinite number of times; I'd gone from one end to the other of those perfectly straight, predictable streets. I'd walked at night, during the day, and even at the time of day when one needs a certain amount of courage to walk through a provincial town: at three in the afternoon, the peak of the siesta, the ghost hour. I'd soaked up the sun in that old amusement park next to the building where the YPF technicians had lived when Cañadón was a prosperous town. I'd spent hours sitting in what could be considered the town square—where spots of green struggle to survive—reading the signs: Protect the plants / Respect the instructions of the caretakers / Don't damage the trees / Use the trash receptacles. I'd emerged exhausted but unharmed by the excess of imperatives. In other words, for days I'd been in frequent contact with the streets; I'd spent hours outside and nothing or nobody had bothered me; I don't think I even crossed paths with anyone. Only very infrequently I thought that something—a hand, an arm, a piece of a person—had just barely pushed aside a curtain from inside a house to watch me pass by. During those days the dogs had also watched me pass and hadn't moved a muscle. They were there, always in groups of ten or more, most of the time asleep, curled up on a street corner. A few times, I'd even gotten close enough to take a picture of the collective reveries of those shabby creatures, a futile attempt to capture the sense of community they exuded even when each roamed who-knows-where in what dream. One or another would manage to open an eye when I stood too close, but that was all; they never reacted to me in any other way. Until the day of the sign, the day when they had to send me their collective message. Enough was enough. They waited for me in a large group on the corner. I saw their fixed stares, their change of attitude. I'm addicted to *Animal Planet*, and am used to deciphering animal behavior. I tried to keep going as if nothing was happening, when one of them, who seemed to be the leader of the pack, gathered momentum and grabbed my ankle between his teeth. I stood still; he wasn't biting, just threatening. My desperation at that moment did not come so much from the bite-in-waiting as the fact that when I looked around—at the line of houses that continued to the south, at the road that leads to Caleta Olivia, at the street that supposedly leads to the city center—I saw nobody, not a single soul.

• • •

Pedro, alias El Bueno, The Good, has a pack of Particulares cigarettes in one hand and a thick chain he holds onto tightly in the other. He uses it to scare off the dogs. It's a lot more effective than the sticks some of his neighbors use, he says, by way of recommendation. The chains don't bounce off their backs. Today is his day off. Though, like everybody else, he ends up doing on that day the same things he does on all the other days. His work fundamentally consists of waiting, and for waiting, there's nothing like a good cigarette. Keeps you company, doesn't talk, doesn't ask questions. El Bueno works for one of the many multinational service providers that opened in the area after the YPF restructuring, a company that does oil-well cementing. He and his team come along after the others have bored the wells and installed the tubing. They pour the cement between the well walls and the tubing, and that's it. That's how specialized everything is these days. There's a long time between when they pour the cement and when it dries—twenty-four, sometimes forty-eight hours. The setting time, they call it. When he's not smoking while he's waiting, El Bueno is watching TV or listening to music. His colleagues, too. Sometimes they talk. Especially when they work in the South, in the Rio Gallegos area, where snow often blocks the roads, and they have to spend days stuck in their little cubicles, totally isolated. His cell phone rings, interrupting him, but Pedro resumes talking without taking a breath. From this corner, like from so many others, you can see the boundaries of Cañadón, the exact spot where the last house surrenders to the desert. The surrounding meseta looks like gray, dense volcanic lava, which at any moment is going to completely bury the town.

That guy over there, running—he points to him—is the delegate from the Union of State Petroleum Workers. It used to be the SUPE, the Sindicato Unido Petrolero del Estado, and after privatization, it became the SUPeH, the Sindicato Unido de Petróleo e Hidrocarburo. The delegate wears gold-framed eyeglasses and is trailed by a little white dog. He always runs at this time of day, that's why he has that body, El Bueno opines. Thin but wiry. It's the second time he runs past this corner, which apparently is part of his circuit. El Bueno lights another cigarette; no, he's not very involved in all that union stuff. And if he were, he wouldn't join the SUPeH but rather Petroleros Privados. The SUPeH is dead, it was our grandfathers' union. The only thing it does now is buy medicine for the company's retirees. The delegate runs by for the third time, like a hamster.

Moving his hands as if they were the blades on a crazed wind-mill, the president of the Cañadón Development Association tells me, in the same hyperbolic style with which he describes his plans to lift the town out of its misery, that he has been forced to propose a Resolution to control the dogs in the town:

—WHEREAS: Because of the uncontrolled increase in the canine population that has led to an increase in incidences of dog bites, some of a serious and traumatic nature, as well as because of dogs loose on the streets, some of whom exhibit aggressive behavior, children and adults are unable to move about freely, either walking or using a bicycle as a means of transportation.

—WHEREAS: Having had the opportunity to receive verbally and in writing a range of opinions from residents, who have raised the problem of "loose dogs on public streets," the conclusion has been reached that in most cases these animals have owners, who, due to ignorance or a lack of awareness of their responsibilities, leave them loose on public streets, causing a range of inconveniences and dangers to the residents, especially those who use the streets of the town.

—WHEREAS: The issue of animal health is intimately connected to human health, for the former can carry many diseases (zoonotic diseases) and can constitute potential dangers to public health. It is essential that we educate people to show respect for the animals and their fellow citizens, as these animals share the town with people . . .

excerpt from Resolution N. 409, Cañadon Seco
Development Association, *November 1, 2002.*

My understanding is that in Cañadón, animals share the town with people and not vice versa, which makes me greatly admire this place and have no desire to leave. I decide to stay a little longer, even if that means a bite or an ambush. A spell doesn't necessarily break instantaneously on both sides, which is where the problem often resides. The dogs give me their message, but I don't want to leave. I remain in the town like those splinters that burrow under the surface of the skin, that can be felt but not found easily enough to remove. I remain like an ingrown nail, obstinate in causing discomfort. What I do these days, so that people don't look at me and dogs don't bite me, is not go outside, practically not move from here, inside. In the town restaurant they let me use a table as if it were my desk, and that's where I spend my days.

Sometimes, very infrequently, someone comes and sits down at my table. They ask me what I'm doing there, surrounded by books and papers, but I always have on the tip of my tongue some questions that save me from answering. What's this about the dogs, for example, I ask Domingo, who sidles up with his beer in hand. Impossible, he tells me. They've become a plague. You can't walk peacefully through town or send the kids out to do an errand. They're starving, that's the problem. And you know what happens with hunger: if it's capable of addling a person's brain, what about an animal's. A plague, that's what they are. And they hold neighborhood meetings, cook up resolutions based on Spanish or Italian regulations, from civilized places, as if this were one as well. But, in the end, the problem doesn't get resolved. There's why they call Cañadón Seco a farmyard, because there are more dogs than people. We have to get rid of all of them, and that's that. In one fell swoop, enough with all this tiptoeing around. I brought up the wrong subject, it seems. I struggle to move on to something else. It's not easy. If a kid can't safely ride a bike, what's the point of living in this town, why be a kid. Domingo's questions overwhelm me. If the bitch has puppies, why not drown them right away, before they even open their eyes. His suggestions do, too. I ask him about his job: that usually works with men. Domingo is part of the administrative staff of an electrical service company. He used to work in the oil fields, installing high tension lines, but he got a hernia and now he's confined to office work. All day surrounded by paperwork and officemates. How can I stand to be surrounded by paper? For him, there's no worse nightmare. At least I don't have officemates, I say, but he doesn't think that's funny. Another plague, he says, narrowing it down. The whole day, talking and complaining. Especially the women. Talking about their private lives, criticizing everybody, even God and the Holy Mary. Before, out in the fields, everybody worked together and that was all there was to it. If they talked, it was to share technical information. Why go around talking about everything? They even have to know when they get their monthlies, how the kids are doing in school. They should get their pay docked for talking, that would shut them up because they're capable of doing anything for a couple of pesos. But he can't say anything because he's new, and the women are already in management. Management! See if they'd be able to reckon with what he used to do before they imprisoned him there, with the paperwork. A plague, that's what they are.

• • •

After that conversation, I almost don't look up. I bury myself in what I have in front of me on my improvised desk. I read more than I write. I'm on Jean-Paul Kauffmann's second book. In the first one, *The Arch of Kerguelen*, Kauffmann recounts the time he spent on the Kerguelens, those isolated and inaccessible islands that are also called, with more explicit toponymy, Desolation Islands. These islands, not even within the Antarctic Region, are capable of frightening people off—literally: he says that even the explorer who first mapped them refused to get off the boat because of the oppressive feeling he got from his view on deck. In the other one, *The Black Room at Longwood*, the one I'm reading now, he recounts the time he spent on Saint Helena trying to perceive, or rather embody, what Napoleon experienced as an English prisoner on that island in the middle of the Atlantic Ocean. For Kauffmann, the remote island and Napoleon are an excuse: both accounts are in fact treatises on captivity.

Before writing those books, Jean-Paul Kauffman worked as a journalist for the magazine *L'Evénement du jeudi*. In May 1985, he arrived in Beirut with Michel Seurat to write an article; they soon became two of the hundreds of Western hostages held in Lebanon during the eighties. The government of Iran and Hezbollah—not yet a party with parliamentary representation—demanded, in exchange for the hostages, that France liberate the fifteen Shia militants and Anis al-Naqqash, who had been arrested in France for attempting to assassinate the ex-prime minister of the Shah of Iran; they also demanded that France stop supporting Iraq, at that time engaged in a war with Iran. Fancy that. So much for international relationships. Michel Seurat died in captivity, and Kauffmann, after being held for three years, returned to his country on May 5, 1988. For those three years, they say, he spent most of the time blindfolded, shackled, starving, and subjected to repeated mock executions. They also say that when Kauffmann landed at the military airport of Villacoublay, everything he experienced was visible on his face, even though he made no public statements. Later, he became the editor of a wine magazine, then a magazine devoted to cigarettes. The carpe diem of someone who saw death up close? I don't think so; rather, a tribute to the senses of taste and smell, the ones that did not abandon him when all the others—such as his mental faculties, his confidence—did. An homage to the animal aspects of his being.

Those senses are also a basic resource in the books that tangentially return to everything that was never stated publicly. "Captivity," he says when he analyzes Napoleon's life on the island prison, "is first of all a smell," an aroma of humiliation, something impossible to communicate. Kauffmann takes up residence on Saint Helena and spends hours at Longwood, the mansion the English gave Napoleon, less to show him that they recognized his rank than to remind themselves of the high-ranking prisoner they had bagged. Kauffmann remains there alone, anxious, ready for his encounter with captivity. He waits for it as if it were a beast he must capture; he can smell it. He reaches the conclusion that all kinds of imprisonment have the same rancid smell. His obsession acts as medium; he concentrates and convokes the spirits that experienced that situation, the specific fear it arouses. The fear of dying, literally, but also of disappearing little by little, disintegrating, turning into a phantom inside an unrecognizable body. To others and to oneself. Kauffmann recovers the voices of those who accompanied Napoleon in exile: the count who was his close collaborator and now wants to turn the past into literature; a baron who hates that count and loves Napoleon with the same passion; another reticent count and his capricious wife; a diplomat accused of embezzlement and his dangerous wife; Napoleon's first valet and helper, Ali, who became Longwood's librarian and wrote his own *Memoires*, which were published in 1926. Kauffmann pauses to analyze the small betrayals, the small grandeurs that circulated among them during their shared sojourn at Longwood, as if imprisonment were a lens that makes visible the minutia of each gesture, each relationship. In his account, when someone speaks, the person narrating usually shines the spotlight on the rising and falling of the small hairs around the mouth more than on what the person to whom the mouth belongs is saying. Focusing one's attention on one such detail also seems to be part of the recipe for survival when there is nothing to look at, nowhere to escape, and no thought that does not devolve into torment. As if what Kauffmann really would like to highlight is the unhinging of the point of view, the distortion of the gaze that suffers captivity. A distortion that, it would seem, is the price one pays in captivity for not dying.

FIVE

Celia and I have been struggling for more than ten minutes to cut up a salt-baked chicken. We can't seem to find the joints, the exact angle at which you need apply only a little pressure with the knife and the whole thing gives way. We fail to find them even though she's a nurse at the hospital in Maquinchao. I always thought that nursing school would include some basic surgical training. A few innocuous exercises, transferable skills that would be practiced on, say, chicken cadavers, just in case somewhere—in the sort of place that is plentiful in the South— there wasn't a surgeon and an emergency cut had to be made. In keeping with one of those compelling occupational hazards, Celia has taken on a secondary role, as assistant, and she has left the task on the operating table to the guidance of someone else, and that someone, in this case, happens to be me. In the end, I have destroyed the chicken; what remains are unrecognizable pieces, meat clinging to bones they don't belong to, breasts indistinguishable from meaty thighs. I prefer it like that: instead of the premeditated malice of the perfect cut, it looks more like the work of someone who had no choice but to act out of hunger and desperation.

On the table, in addition to the destroyed chicken, there's a Paraguayan soup and a collection of Arabic dishes: kebbe, falafel, tabouli, baklava, mshabak, hummus. And, those of us sitting around the table: Celia; Carina, a doctor at the Maquinchao hospital; Carmen, a psychologist at the Maquinchao hospital; Clara, the owner of the house we are in and of Ramos Generales Grocery Store; Saul, her cousin who lives out in the county but is visiting today; and I. This morning I entered the grocery store to ask where the Vasca Store was, which is where they sell tickets for the only bus that travels through the southern part of Río Negro Province, and now it's four in the afternoon and I'm still here, sitting at a round table. I left the house only once briefly with Clara before noon to get my stuff from the hotel and buy something at the food fundraiser being held at the hospital. We returned here with three lunch guests— who live together because they recently arrived from different provinces in the North—and the array of Arabic dishes. Clara went to high school in Buenos Aires and Punta del Este; then she got married and came here to take over the family land and this grocery store her grandfather had established. Her sister, on the other hand, didn't; she stayed in Buenos Aires, studying plant genetics and traveling regularly to Germany to present her research. Clara is one of those women who assumes ownership of a town, a character who has influence over everything that is said and done in a place; a bit like Faulkner's Emily, but without the tragedy. Needless to say, she rules over the table. The doctor, perhaps in order to establish a counterpoint, becomes meticulous about epicurean issues, such as how to drink wine, how to cut cheese. There's something dense about her, undigested. The psychologist, who's sitting on my right, says, no, obviously she doesn't treat middle class neurotics who must choose between the armchair and the couch. Carmen tells me that she works in mental health in Río Negro, where there's a totally revolutionary law regarding the treatment of those whose illness can be placed under the rubric "madness." The idea is to de-institutionalize the mentally ill, a project that aims to do away with insane asylums.

In order to understand the de-institutionalization of the mentally ill, we must first understand the cultural process of institutionalization. The insane asylum is an established institutional form, visible and terminal, of a cultural illness . . . the culture of mortification, in which the subject is being coerced and is on the verge of being suppressed as a thinking subject. The indicators of this coercion are: a) the disappearance of courage, b) the disappearance of the intellect, stupefaction, people who have no clear idea about what they are doing . . . c) the disappearance of joy. There is no criticism or self-criticism. What prevails are the symptoms that fail to be seen as protest. Individuals come to depend more on their weaknesses and on displaying them . . . than on protesting. There is no such thing as transgression, only infractions. Transgression in itself is foundational: for the raising of consciousness, for revolutionary theory, et cetera; on the other hand, infraction is not foundational for anything: it is the municipal code.

from "Conference debates about deinstitutionalization,"
Fernando Ulloa, Zona Erógena magazine, No. 14

Carmen explains: the idea is to do away with the system of institutionalization of the mentally ill, for it isn't a cure but rather a means of controlling the affliction, and instead to re-socialize the afflicted by integrating them into the labor market. Of course, if someone has an episode, they will have the support of the hospital, which is where she, Carmen, works. But they are treated there as they would be if they had appendicitis: once the inflammation is reduced, the person returns home. Efforts to support the people suffering from these ailments and that are, therefore, on the path to healing, she continues, have been brought together under what here in Río Negro is called Empresas Sociales, or Social Services. According to this framework, patients with psychosis or schizophrenia, for example, can work on farms, in greenhouses, cultural centers, hotels.

"Hotels?"

"Yes, hotels."

At least I didn't run off with my boss's money, I think, while I confirm that, apparently, the person who mapped out the spheres of activities was not a Hitchcock enthusiast. Only in Trieste, of all places in the world, is this law being enforced, Carmen tells me, which manages to give me even more goose bumps. Something tells me that in Trieste, hospitals, the labor market, policies, and politicians, among other things, make things much more feasible than in Río Negro. I'm about to ask Carmen if, considering the state of our public policies, this law might not be a freefall into the abyss, but I realize that everybody at the table has already moved on to another subject. More than one hundred Turks disappeared over a five-year period, Clara's cousin says.

• • •

During the first decades of the twentieth century, many settlers emigrated to this part of Río Negro from the Levant, which more or less corresponds to present-day Lebanon and Syria. In Maquinchao half a century ago, a Lebanese Association was founded, which still exists today, and one of its members was Clara's grandfather, a "Turk," as those in the South call the inhabitants of territories that were under Turkish control for four centuries. The thing is, nobody reacted quickly enough, the cousin continues, as if he were picking up a conversation that only he remembers; if they'd done something sooner it might not have reached that number, that level of savagery. At the time, they'd get here however they could; they'd make it to Neuquén or even Roca, and from there, where some of their more established compatriots had their own general stores, they would load merchandise into a sulky, a cart, whatever they could find, and take off across the meseta to sell or barter their goods. They usually went out in pairs: a Turk and a peon. I look at all the faces around the table: nobody is bothered that their cousin of Lebanese grandparents is using this term. They would get lost out there, spend months roaming from one place to another. They would say that this semi-desert region reminded them of over there, where they came from. That helped, probably, because things were not at all easy. They had to sleep out in the open and walk all day—in the cold, the heat, whatever there was. And deal with the Indians, who were sometimes easy and other times hard as rock. And all that, without a word from their families, nothing. Totally cut off, the one from the other. Often the peon was born here and then they wouldn't even be able to talk to each other, though in solitude like that, signs are more quickly understood, they say. They would come across a group that was starting to build the railroad and then, at least, even though they didn't understand much, they had some good customers, a group to share a meal with, human sounds. They weren't used to that much solitude; normally they lived surrounded by cousins, siblings, family, and that's what they wanted to get back to as soon as possible. The table set and everyone sitting around it. And a lot to eat, to serve. Because that's how they'd been brought up. They weren't like the Bedouins, who were nomadic, who lived like that; they were used to having a house, a place of their own, and in the end, they crossed the ocean only to end up living like Bedouins. No, it wasn't easy. But they did it with the idea of saving enough money to start their own businesses, like their compatriots, who gave them merchandise on consignment. They'd wander around the meseta, thinking about the store that awaited them in the future and the family that was waiting for them now. Maybe even some of them had a good time. You never know. The point is they left, and once they'd left, months would pass before they'd return to Roca or Neuquén to pay what they owed and load up their carts again. It could be one, two, five months, depending on many things: the time of year, the mood of the Indians, what people needed in the hamlets. That's why everybody in town had gotten used to not expecting them on any specific date: one day they'd simply show up. That's why, the cousin repeats, it took so long to find out about the massacre. When the first ones didn't return, people thought that business had been bad, that it was taking them two, maybe three months to sell what they normally sold in one. Anybody who works in sales knows that: traveling or not, in 1910 or now. So, they thought that they'd been de-

layed, but that they'd return. Others thought they'd run off to
Chile, and that was that, only God would ever pay their coun-
trymen back for their merchandise. Until one person refused
to believe either of those things, either that it would take two
years to sell what they could carry in that broken-down cart, or
that his own brother-in-law would be capable of running off to
Chile with the goods they'd given him. His name was Salomon
Daud: he was the one who first went to the authorities.

In El Cuy, Department 9 de Julio of the Argentine
Territory of Río Negro, on the fifteenth day of April
of the year nineteen hundred and nine, at three in
the afternoon, Salomon Daud, of Arabic nationality,
aged twenty-nine, married, merchant, resident of this
district, a person known to the undersigned commissioner, states as follows:

—His brother-in-law, José Elías, accompanied
by an Arab peon by the last name of Ezen, left in the
month of August of the year nineteen hundred and
seven from General Roca, carrying merchandise to
sell throughout that department, and accompanied by
four mules, of ownership unknown, though one was a
sorrel, owned by Miguel Muñoz. As they have not yet
returned and no news has been heard from them, he
suspects that his brother-in-law and Ezen have been
murdered and requests that the police take measures
to discover the real reason for their disappearance . . .

—José Elías is of Arab extraction, born in Syria,
son of Elías Noti and María Agustín, twenty-two years
old, single, uneducated, of normal height, with a flat

nose, dark brown curly hair, thin beard and mustache, known to speak loudly and quickly, also known to dress moderately well and with his hat pushed back on his head.

Testimony from Case N. 1875, consisting of four parts with more than nine hundred pages regarding the robberies and murders that occurred in the area of Paraje Lagunitas between 1905 and 1910.

It seems that after the complaint was filed, Superintendent Torino, of the police station in El Cuy, received direct orders from the police commissioner and governor of the territory, Carlos Gallardo, to find out if there was anything to Daud's suspicions. At first, so as not to stir up too much trouble, he sent a spy of sorts, a civilian disguised as a somewhat forsaken gaucho, to prowl around the camps where the suspects lived and see what he could discover. And what he found, Daud's son finally recounted many years later, left his mother in tears for the rest of her life.

It seems that a gang had settled near Lagunitas that lived off what they could steal from the traveling salesmen. So as not to leave a trace, they'd kill them before robbing them. They did everything as a group: they'd gather in the tent of one of the gang members, and when the poor peddler was relaxed, eating and drinking, they'd kill him right there, along with his helper, with one bullet or as many as it took. Then they'd distribute among them everything in the cart, for their own use or, as some also say, to sell to the few stores in the area around Lagunitas. Others say they smuggled the merchandise into Chile and sold it there, because one of the gang's head honchos, Juan Cuya, lived with the sister of the man who appeared to be the supreme leader, Pablo Brebáñez, who in turn was the magistrate of the Chilean subdelegación of Toltén, north of Valdivia. Finally Torino caught up with them and discovered that they had killed approximately one hundred and thirty peddlers. Torino managed to capture eighty gang members, more or less; before he arrived a few had already escaped to Chile: the leaders, the head honchos, as usual. Clara's cousin says, yes, he would also like a cup of Turkish coffee. Once they were dead, they decapitated them and cut open their chests to remove their hearts because, according to Antonia Gueche—alias Macagua, the woman who was the sorceress and healer of the gang and who, two decades earlier, had served in the ranks of the army in Roca, dressed as a man—it was good to dry those hearts because they gave them "courage to kill Turks and Christians." At other times, and to the same purpose, they ate them instead of saving them for later. Also, to provide them with protection and courage, they kept the penises. Then they burned the remains in order to leave no trace. Some of the gang members asserted that the bones ground to dust also offered protective powers, so they would always grab a handful.

I will show you fear in a handful of dust.

The Wasteland, *T. S. Eliot*

In his book, *Departures Without Return: Arabs in Patagonia*, Elías Chucair recounts the incidents in Lagunitas through the direct testimonies that appear in the case file. That book is one of the many that Chucair has written about this region of Patagonia. He has one central hypothesis, as well as several peripheral ones: the traveling salesmen of Arabic origin were massacred by a gang of indigenous people who were mostly Chileans and even "constituted something like a Chilean invasion." The same was said by several newspapers at the time, but it occurs to me that the hypothesis of a conflict between nation states seems forced when one considers how evanescent the idea of belonging to a nation—Chile or Argentina—would have been for a group of people who were, in large part, of Mapuche origin, and who, after the military campaigns waged by both Argentina and Chile to annex those territories just three decades earlier, did not feel any belonging to either. They were, rather, pariahs of the borderlands. Moreover, though perhaps the leader of the gang was Chilean and they were effectively based in Chile, everything leads one to believe that they were less inspired by geopolitics than by ambition for illicit wealth. To pursue this goal, they were perfectly positioned: he was an official near a border where the authorities supposedly in charge of enforcing the law—customs agents and police forces—were scarce (in the second case) or definitively absent (in the first; customs enforcement in the area became functional in Bariloche only after a decade later). Might Chucair's hypothesis be part of one of those chain reactions that always occurs among the xenophobes of this world, whereby a group discriminated against by others defends itself by discriminating against a third, and thereby successively? Even at the risk of over-psychologizing, I ask Chucair if his emphasis on the Chilean origin of the crimes is not his response, as a descendent of Arabs, to the xenophobia that Patagonia has exhibited toward his people.

• • •

"No, absolutely not," he answers when I interview him at his house in Ingeniero Jacobacci, a town less than one hundred kilometers from Maquinchao. *He* never felt that discrimination. However, throughout all of Patagonia, not only in the Andean part, it's common to encounter the underlying suspicion that the Arabs—"Turks"—made their money cheating Indians, using the most refined techniques of the souk against counterparts who were mere babes in the art of the barter. There's a joke that makes the rounds of bars in Patagonia: "You know why there's a town in the province of Buenos Aires that's called Indio Rico? Because no Turk ever came through there." There are also sayings, such as "as large as a Turk's linens," which makes reference to the enormous amount of things that the traveling salesmen supposedly got from the Indians in exchange for a bag of yerba maté or a bottle of caña, for example, and that they then wrapped in a piece of cloth they would spread out on the ground as soon as they arrived at any hamlet or camp. That's what they say in the South; I heard such things throughout my childhood. When I left Chucair, the day I interviewed him in Jacobacci, I took a few turns around that peaceful town that to Theroux seemed like the antechamber to death. I entered a restaurant where some men were sitting around one table while all the rest of the tables were empty. I asked them, after a while, if any of them knew anything about the massacre of Turks in the Lagunitas area. They all knew about it, even though almost a century had passed. One of them, who works for INTA, the National Agricultural Technology Institute, and frequently travels throughout the region, told me that around there, around Lagunitas, they say that they were all tall tales, exaggerations, that what really happened is that the peddlers ran off with the merchandise and sold everything in Chile.

Yet another example of the struggle between civilization and barbarism, said the newspapers of the time. This threat to a particular community disrupted the plans of the Argentinean government at that time to encourage immigration, and sullied the image of a welcoming republic, which they tried to spread around the world precisely for the year of the centennial celebration. Maybe for that reason, among others, it was convenient to insist on the "Chilean" nature of the crimes.

Los horrores de los bandoleros

Chilenos del Cuy

Importante captura de una gavilla de bandoleros — Crímenes horribles —¡Asesinos y antropófago ! - Los horrores del desierto Asesinatos sistemáticos—Horrible disciplina de la gavilla!! - Se mata á los compañeros heridos! - Los tormentos de las víctimas.

Neuquen, 29 de Enero de 1910

A cuarente leguas de la Colonia Rosa sobre el Río Negro, á 30 de la capital del Neuquen, sobre la ribera de esta del Río Limay existe una vasta al irlandese desierta denominada «la Travesía», paraje árido, montañoso, con población muy escasa compuesta en parte de indios vaqueanos y en parte de chilenos, que desde la cordillera vienen avanzando para poblar las tierras todavía fiscales del territorio de Río Negro

Hace dos años esos chilenos poblaron los contrafuertes andinos, pero las continuas compras de campos fiscales por particulares concluyeron con las pocas

THE HORRORS OF THE BANDITS
Chileans from Cuy

Important arrest of a gang of bandits — Horrific crimes — Murderers and Cannibals! — Horrors in the desert. Systematic massacres — The gangs' horrific punishments — Wounded fellow gang members murdered — Victims tortured.

Neuquen, 29 January 1910

The pen resists describing the horrific acts committed by those bandits, who are more savage, more ferocious, than all the uncivilized peoples of Africa. They cut off their ears, their tongues, their fingers and hands, then burned them. They even cut open their chests and pulled out their hearts.

But that wasn't enough; they roasted their intestines in order to discover the difference between the flesh of a Turk and the flesh of a Christian.

After committing these horrific acts of cannibalism that offend twentieth-century civilization, they burned the corpses and threw the ashes to the wind . . .

All of that, just to steal the hundred or two hundred pesos the poor victims had earned with so much hard work . . . !

The least the national government can do for those remote territories is give them enough police forces to prevent the repetition of such acts, which destroy our status as a civilized nation, in our own eyes and in the eyes of foreigners.

Bahía Blanca *newspaper, January 29, 1910*

ECOS DEL DIA

LA SEGURIDAD EN LOS TERRITORIOS

País de inmigración y de bandolerismo

La República Argentina es país esencialmente de inmigración, como que el que más trascendental de sus problemas es la población. Este es precepto aceptado desde las primeras horas de la nacionalidad, auspiciado por el gran Alberdi y reconocido por gobernantes y estadistas como la más importante preocupación del presente y del porvenir.

Los territorios nacionales, fondo de reserva de la economía del país y futuros estados de vida propia, tienen que ser poblados por la inmigración, que es la que va a resolver el problema étnico y la que va a definir nuestra grandeza.

Ahora bien; ¿es presumible que la inmigración guíe sus pasos hacia el Neuquén cuando sabe, porque la prensa nacional lo dice y la prensa extranjera lo repite, que allí no hay garantías para la vida, que la policía no existe como defensa eficaz y que los bandoleros cometen depredaciones, asaltan establecimientos y roban los tesoros de los Bancos?

NEWS OF THE DAY
SECURITY IN
THE TERRITORIES

———

A nation of immigration and banditry

———

The Republic of Argentina, whose most significant problem is population, is essentially a country of immigrants. Since the first days of the nation, this has been the operating principle, expressed by the great Alberdi and acknowledged by leaders and statesmen as the most important concern of the present and the future.

The nation's territories, the reserve fund of its economy and its future, states in their own rights, must be populated by immigrants, thereby solving our ethnic problem and defining our greatness.

However, can we presume that immigrants will make their way to Neuquén when it is known, because the national press says so and the foreign press repeats it, that there are no security guarantees there, that the police are nonexistent as an efficient defense against the bandits who commit depredations, attack institutions, and rob from the banks?

So said *La Nueva Provincia* newspaper on February 6, 1910. It went on to say:

How can the brutality in Río Negro be an inducement for immigrants? With heavy hearts we ourselves read stories about the horrible outrage of that endless series of murders recently discovered in El Cuy, with a plethora of such terrifying and brutal details. Is it possible for people to disappear and for such loathsome murders to become the norm in a civilized country, for years to pass and nobody notice the disappearance of those poor people who ventured into those regions . . . ?

In the face of these events, which send us back to primitive epochs and gainsay our notable progress in spreading abroad a favorable idea of our country so that we receive a vigorous flow of immigrants and offer them all the benefits of well-being and remunerative work; in the face of this we assert that the opinion foreigners hold of us will necessarily lead to depressing consequences.

Our national government must understand that it is perfectly absurd to spend twenty million pesos on anniversary celebrations when a third of the republic lacks a police force that is capable of protecting the lives of its inhabitants.

And it should further understand that we cannot promote immigration by exhibiting brutal savagery, precisely in those regions where foreign labor will be needed to collaborate in the social and economic progress required to uphold our national identity.

This is still a country of immigration and banditry, one hundred years after its birth into the cradle of the civilized world.

Who would have thought: *La Nueva Provincia*, one of the newspapers that most actively defended State terrorism during the last Argentine dictatorship in the nineteen seventies, wondering if it's possible that people can simply disappear and loathsome murders can become the norm in a civilized country.

In keeping with the tradition of Patagonia's unaddressed grievances against the central government, police reinforcements to deal with this case never arrived. Its resolution remained solely in the hands of José María Torino—police superintendent in the nearest town, El Cuy—for whom things did not go well at all. Seven months after what he thought would be his most heroic deed, his most triumphant act, he ended up in prison, along with all the others. "Dear Sister," he writes on October 11, 1910, from the prison in Viedma. It's not easy to continue; it's not easy to write this letter from hell to explain to his family that he is not a thief or a murderer. He shuts his eyes to think about how to begin, how to be clear without worrying them— his sister, his father, his wife, his children—and the only thing that comes to him are those images. The same ones that prevent him from falling asleep when he finally throws himself down on that putrid cot in his cell. Those days of the convoy, that's what's stuck in his head. Except: sometimes he tries to quell those images by conjuring up the face of his little boy or picturing one of those rare winter days there in El Cuy, when it snows, and the ground and the pond are all white. But no, it's futile. These images are immediately swept away and again he sees them, sees himself: he has managed to capture those bastards and now he's taking them, with the help of a few assistants and volunteers who joined him along the way, on the road from Lagunitas to Fort General Roca, where he plans to hand them over to the chief of police. There are about eighty, out of which eight are women. They are on horseback, their hands tied, their eyes downcast, not talking. It was forbidden: he forbade it. He had to take all possible precautions; those murderers had shown that nothing intimidated them and, anyway, there were many more of them than of him and his improvised posse. Any revolt had a good chance of success. He could not allow himself to get distracted for even a second. He had to remain vigilant, permanently vigilant. And so he did for the twenty-two days it took for them to get there. Not a moment of distraction. His level of concentration was such that he didn't even feel the exhaustion, or the heat, or the disgust that whole gang of vermin provoked in him. Nothing. The only thing that went through his head was his duty to make sure they got what they deserved. He couldn't even imagine the moment they'd reach Roca and everybody would be there: the whole town assembled and even some others who'd come from neighboring towns, and journalists from Bahía and journalists from Buenos Aires. Everybody there to see the cannibals, and he, there, leading the convoy of scum. No, he didn't think about that: and even now he can't, now that he is merely another prisoner, he can't make that moment of glory stick in his head. "Dear Sister:" No. What is stuck is the trek along the meseta, the handcuffed murderers, and the silence. Nobody spoke: not they and not the others. Twenty-two days like that, twenty-two days that were an eternity, like one of those treks that pilgrims say changes their lives. They could be on the move for only five hours a day, at the most. Because of exhaustion, because of the sun, but above all because he had to organize each maneuver with extreme caution. He had them dismount two at a time, never more. That's the only way he could be certain there wouldn't be a revolt, and he watched to make sure that they didn't signal to one another or communicate in any other way. Two by two they got off their horses while the others waited. That took a long time: three, four hours. Every day, the same way, over and over, without ever breaking the rules. And now he turns out to be just one more of them, because they have him locked away there in Viedma, along with all that refuse. He knows what they are: he entered their camp, he saw their faces when they confessed. He smelled their taste for death. He penetrated the desert and walked with all those beasts breathing down his neck. He advanced at the slowest possible pace, surrounded by beasts who wanted to attack him from behind. Not for a single instant did he allow fear to hurry him along, to force him to ruin everything. Nobody can know what that's like. The courage you have to muster to withstand that land and that silence and the breath of those threatened beasts, exuding hatred. "Dear Sister:" He would like to know if there was ever another police superintendent in the history of the nation who carried out his duty so faithfully and received what he received in exchange. But he's not going to start the letter like that: he must be precise and decisive. Communicate the news, his circumstances, not his mood. Much less ask the question that he asks himself every day. Sometimes, he wakes up in the middle of the night and can't believe it. That he's there, like this, accused of the deaths of half his prisoners, who, they say, died from the blows of sabers, rifles, and the restraints he and his men put them in. Such slander. If that's what had happened, if he'd turned over his prisoners in such a state, why didn't the director of the jail denounce him previously, why didn't those bastards he arrested denounce him, why did they wait six months to say the things they're saying now. Abuse of authority? Infamy. Abuse was what they did, what they are doing to him, that gang of judges and prosecutors determined to place obstacles in the way of the truth. They brought him here, to Viedma, in second-class train cars, they forbade him from ordering food at the restaurant on the train, and they forced him to make do with crumbs. The entire way surrounded by the prisoners he himself had captured and their continuous threats and taunts, their pestilent odor. Everybody under the same conditions. They die, of course prisoners die; he knows why they die, because now he's in the same situation. But not because of what those scoundrels say, God knows they didn't die because of him, who made it to headquarters because he knew how to behave, always intrepidly but also with respect and prudence. Not from blows of the saber or anything else; they die because in all those prisons, in the one in Viedma and in the others, they put twenty of them in two-by-two cells, like coffins, without any ventilation at all. They don't even have floors, not even wood planks, at the very least, to stop the damp from rising from the dirt and giving them all tuberculosis and legs crippled from rheumatism. And they die because when these and other diseases are continually attacking them—which they actually deserve, not like him—nobody does anything. Not the directors of the prisons, not the judges, not the prosecutors. Not them and not that veterinarian they bring here to falsify the autopsy reports—because he doesn't fool anybody with his pathetic pretense of being a doctor. They spent all winter without any medicine, without even a blanket, no fur wraps as he himself deserved. These prisons are a torment. He can't say that, either; he must simply spell out the facts with all the objectivity he can muster, because he was always vigilant, and he continues to be, "Dear Sister, . . ."

• • •

Nilo Fulvi, director of the Viedma Historical Archives, was the person who saved from the flames the files that contain the statements of the murderers and the witnesses, the letter Superintendent Torino wrote to his sister, the letter the priest in Viedma wrote to Torino's father to tell him that if he didn't do something to get him out of the Viedma prison, he believed, or rather, he was certain, José Torino's life would be in serious danger. Nilo Fulvi says that in spite of the priest's letter, Torino spent four more years in that prison, and nothing is known about what happened to him afterwards. And he explains to me that, after poring through the files, he concluded that a mere two years after the arrests, in 1912, the case was closed. In the meantime, there were a series of irregularities that Fulvi lists and among which include: many months without any decision regarding the status of those who'd been arrested; the unusual turnover of judges presiding over the case; the decision of the prosecutor, Vicente Villafañe, to not file charges and to recommend that the case be closed because "there is no proof of the presence of the Syrians and their attackers in the places they were said to have been murdered"; and because, among other things, "the departure of the Syrians from General Roca 'to the south,' as claimed by the relatives of the victims, does not conclusively prove that they went to the region of Sierra Negra and Lagunitas." Nilo Fulvi, who not only rescued the files but also read them and analyzed them carefully, asserts that he finds it difficult to believe that ruling by the prosecutor, which clearly disregarded abundant evidence and a plethora of fully concordant testimonies, confessions of the accused, and witness statements. It was so flawed, he continues, that the judge himself felt obliged to refer to an article in the Criminal Code, according to which a judge who is not in agreement with a ruling by the prosecutor can request he be replaced by a "special prosecutor." The one appointed for this case was Emilio De Rege, and the ruling he made after having analyzed the case are the paragraphs that Nilo Fulvi quotes: "Nobody, absolutely nobody, has seriously concerned himself with this trial from the day it left the hands of the investigating superintendent . . . since it passed to the court, that is, since November 1909 (stated with all due respect), not a single diligence was carried out in pursuit of a clarification of the important facts, which at one point was of interest not only to this country but also to all nations who send their immigrants to this country. It is not, Your Honor, only a matter of not clarifying the facts in a timely fashion, but also that evidence has been destroyed . . . Only on December 9, 1911, after I, the undersigned, was named special prosecutor, and after I studied the voluminous proceedings, did I feel the need to see those pieces of evidence before issuing a ruling on a trial of such momentous importance; and I requested a viewing of the same on December 20, 1911 . . . On April 23 of the current year instructions were given for me to see said evidence, and to my surprise, I was told on May 2 by the certified actuary that all the evidence had disappeared, ordered to be burned by the territorial judge,

Dr. Torres." After asserting that this appears to be a crime, De Rege concludes that, in the absence of any evidence, he has no choice but to request dismissal.

It's incredible, Nilo Fulvi says, that at least he managed to prevent them from burning the evidence that proved that they had burned the evidence. His suspicion, like those of many others regarding the case, is that there was a specific reason no charges were brought and that the case was closed as soon as possible. What that reason is and where it originated is open to the most varied hypotheses. Among them: that when a Chilean magistrate became implicated, the Argentinean government wanted to avoid adding more ink to the sprawling border treaty that dates back to the nineteenth century and for which both governments had sought British arbitration not long before; that they, the local authorities, had caved in to bribes and pressure from local merchants implicated in the case, who were not at all happy that their shops, located in those desert hamlets, were faced with competition from peddlers; that there had been a consensus, as much within the national government as within the territorial government of Río Negro, to conceal any events that would rekindle—precisely when the country was engaged in yet another attempt to join the club of civilized nations—the misunderstanding initiated by Darwin regarding the cannibalism of indigenous Patagonians.

• • •

This is the room, with high ceilings and looking out on what could be called an interior courtyard if it weren't so enormous, that Clara gave me for my stay in Maquinchao. It has completely white walls and two twin beds with shiny iron bedposts, which could very easily be hospital beds. I close the door and only then do I feel at home. I lie down on the bed closest to the window, and I see on the bedside table several books, four to be exact: two cookbooks, a book by Michael Crichton, and another by Thomas Harris, *Red Dragon*. I had seen, inevitable as it knew how to make itself, *The Silence of the Lambs*, and even *Hannibal*, but I'd never read this novel in which Harris brings his cannibalistic psychiatrist into the world. On the back of the book it says that *Red Dragon* was published seven years before his character, Hannibal Lecter, was made so popular by the movie, and also on the book jacket of this post-hit Spanish edition, a blurb by Stephen King states that "Hannibal is Count Dracula for the computer-and-cell-phone age." I open it, just to help me fall asleep, and I find a former FBI agent who receives a visitor one day at his beach house, where he has retired after his glorious capture of Hannibal Lecter left him in a hospital bed, struggling against an almost certain death. The intruder is Jack Crawford, his former boss on that case and in another equally grisly one, who tells him that there have been other murders with chilling similarities to those that only he had been able to solve. That's why, he swears, he had nobody else to turn to. Crawford is convinced that Graham, this agent who now spends his time fixing outboard motors in the Florida Keys, has a special nose for monsters.

A few pages later I learn that the murders are the handiwork of Francis Dolarhyde, a serial killer obsessed with his grandmother's dentures and William Blake. And who, like Hannibal, likes human flesh. Also like the members of the gang I have not stopped hearing about for the last few days. I stay up reading till dawn. Dolarhyde chews his victims for several reasons. One of them, the one most influenced by twentieth-century psychology, points as much to the irreparable wound his mother inflicted on him when she abandoned him as a child as the horror produced in him from living with a grandmother with buck teeth, who, for the slightest offense, would place his penis between open scissors and threaten to close them. But he also chews his victims, the novel says, to assuage the fear they cause him and, above all, to obtain power that he doesn't have. That's why there's nobody he wants to eat as much as Hannibal, who, as the story progresses, is revealed to be the true hero. Isn't this exactly what was assumed by those who roasted the Arab peddlers and ate them? That the Turks' hearts and guts would give them power, courage, "make them handsome"? Isn't this more or less what the most famous cannibals of our time have confessed, the one in Milwaukee and the one in Rotenburg? The need for power and protection, and the desire to devour another, seems to be a combination capable of transcending cultural and chronological differences, even surpassing psychological explanations and criminal justice sentencing.

Armin Meiwes, dubbed the Cannibal of Rotenburg, was a computer repair technician who posted an online ad for men who were willing to be killed and eaten. He hoped he could thereby fulfill a desire he'd had since adolescence, for more than twenty years. The most difficult part, it seems, was to choose among the two hundred applicants who responded to his ad. Once he settled on the Berlin engineer who rang his doorbell one afternoon in March 2001, the rest was simple: the engineer offered no resistance and had no qualms. The first thing he did was ask Meiwes to cut off his penis: he hoped thereby to have the most intense experience of his life. Then they ate it together. Meiwes videotaped the whole thing in order to avoid subsequent misunderstandings. They both enjoyed it, and perhaps through that act the Berlin engineer was attempting to show all of us neurotics who devour ourselves day in and day out that there's no point in continuing to use so many euphemisms. Then, the engineer agreed for Meiwes to carry on with the rest of it, or him, because some things cannot be accomplished à deux: his throat was slashed, he was frozen, and he became the computer technician's main source of nutrition for the following few weeks. Keeping in mind that this story took place in the Northern Hemisphere, he might even have appeared on the spring menu. The day the court in Kassel ruled that Meiwes would be sentenced to eight and a half years of prison for manslaughter, he stated that his strongest desire, above and beyond all others, was to establish a close and permanent relationship with another person. Something that would offer him "safety and protection."

This is the same thing Jeffrey Dahmer, the Milwaukee Cannibal, said, this time in English: that what he wanted more than anything was to be close to someone—best-case scenario, a well-built and submissive white man—who would always be waiting for him when he returned home from work, who would do nothing but wait for him, without seeing anybody or spending his time doing anything else. A captive, permanent companion, someone who would make him feel less alone. That was why, when he saw that his one-night stands always went back to their own lives the following morning, he started to kill them. Once the momentary excitement of having his first victim under his control had passed, however, he realized that the dead didn't really satisfy him, either. At that point he started bringing men to his house to conduct an experiment: first he drugged them and then, with a drill, he made holes in their head into which he injected, with a kitchen syringe, an acid that would penetrate the cavities in their brain. By doing this, he hoped to be able to keep their bodies alive and their minds dead, obedient. But the experiment didn't work, so he killed the seventh one, cut his heart into pieces, and stored the pieces in the freezer; eating a little bit at a time gave him the sensation that the other was becoming part of him. They were becoming one, and he was in control, he couldn't ask for anything more. He did the same thing with several of his subsequent victims. When they caught him, the freezer still held, untasted, the perfectly cut-up heart of his seventeenth victim.

Jeffrey Dahmer gives these first-hand details and many more to Robert K. Ressler, who interviews him to the point of exasperation for his book, *I Have Lived in the Monster*. Ressler, who, ever since childhood, had wanted to know what went on in the minds of murderers, worked for the FBI for twenty years and became an expert in murders committed by people whom he himself named *serial killers*. In his book he says that after several years of contemplating the criminal mind, he can make José Martí's words his own: "I have lived in the monster." Robert

Ressler also advised Thomas Harris when he wrote the novel that has me here, still awake, at four o'clock in the morning. As *Red Dragon* continues, I realize that Dolarhyde cannot be the protagonist of the novel precisely because he lacks the skills necessary to be a monster for our age: he is fragile and neurotic, has psychological problems that torment him and unbounded terror that leads him at moments to lose control and end up overpowered by a Double—the Red Dragon—whom he has unknowingly created. In Dolarhyde there are aspects of a nineteenth-century monster: a Dr. Jekyll and Mr. Hyde. In fact, his last name evokes the pair. The dragon, who at first seemed to be his ally, even a product of his Art—just as Hyde first seemed to Jekyll to be a product of his Science—finally takes over completely, issuing orders from the top of the staircase of his big house, like his toothy grandmother. The twentieth century is over, Harris seems to be saying, and a different profile needs to be created: monsters inspired in the nineteenth century have their own limitations, have lost their strength. Harris, who spent ten years reporting on crime for the Associated Press in New York before becoming a writer and was therefore in constant contact with tormented and defeated men, perhaps realized when he walked into the newsroom one day that it was not in his section where he would find inspiration for his most important character but rather in *Politics* or *International News*. The real monsters of this century parade through those pages, wearing designer suits and giving slickly spun speeches. Hannibal, apart from his power of irony, is most like them: he never loses control or feels tormented, no matter what he does. Lecter recognizes that he takes great pleasure in killing, a pleasure that he assumes God also feels, judging only from the news they sometimes allow him to read in prison. The fact that they have imprisoned him for having indulged in that pleasure speaks only to the error, that is, the terror, of others. His interpretations as a seasoned psychiatrist protect him, convince him that it is these men and their fears, their euphemisms, who misunderstand everything and act in consequence. How could he feel remorse? Nor does he lose control for a single instant: he is capable of killing his victims and simultaneously describing to them exactly what is happening to their arteries, their blood, their heart, and their pulmonary functions at the precise instant the knife point penetrates five centimeters from their spine. Once imprisoned, he is capable of withstanding without any alteration the humiliations and privations (especially of his books) to which he has been subjected by Dr. Chilton, the director of Chesapeake State Hospital for the Criminally Insane, where he is imprisoned. Shackled and deprived of all his possessions, he is also capable of driving that same director crazy with just one of his scathing comments. And he has even been capable of avoiding prison, which is what the law ordains for those who do not lose control while they commit their crimes, an achievement neither the Cannibal of Rotenburg nor the Milwaukee Cannibal could boast. In Germany it was determined that Meiwes could not go to an asylum because "although he suffers from a serious psychic anomaly, he is fully responsible for his actions." In Wisconsin, in spite of the defense Robert Ressler recommended to prove that Dahmer had lost his mind by the time he committed his last murders, the jury decided that "a person, to be considered mentally ill, must behave as such most of the time . . . hence Dahmer was in his right mind when he committed those crimes." He was given fifteen life sentences, the equivalent of 936 years in prison, but everything was resolved much sooner, because in March 1994, he was beaten to death in the prison bathroom by another prisoner serving a life sentence, one Christopher Scarver. "In my opinion," Ressler wrote in *I Have Lived in the Monster*, "neither Dahmer nor Scarver should have been in a prison; but both should have been permanent residents of a mental institution." I think tomorrow I'll ask Carmen what she thinks about this, and I continue to read Harris's book.

• • •

Will Graham, the former FBI agent, cannot refuse his colleague's offer to work on this case. He agrees, even though this threatens the stability of his relationship as well as the equilibrium of his life, which has been cobbled back together, even though it means once again having to deal with the smell of rotting corpses, autopsies, the conflicts between the FBI and local police forces, reheated coffee served in little plastic cups, and sleepless nights facing a pile of facts that fail to offer him a clue. But none of that is what really worries him; what terrifies him is knowing ahead of time that in order to find that clue and catch this new murderer, he will have to, at some point, turn to Hannibal. And knowing that Hannibal will not only give him the clue but tell him what he never wanted to hear: how similar they are. Both have spent time in a psychiatric institution, time in a hospital bed, both feel pleasure when they kill though they acknowledge it to different degrees and express it in different ways, and, fundamentally, both are capable of exercising total control over others. Why? Because, as Hannibal tells him as soon as he has the chance, both have an imagination that makes them capable of adapting any point of view, and because they know how to tolerate the fear that this entails. The threat of a breakdown, the loss of one's internal axis. That's why Hannibal the Great respects Graham, because he's capable of entering the minds of others and, at the same time, preventing anybody else from entering his. He's not like so many others, like Dr. Chilton himself, who, when he thinks he's analyzing Lecter, is actually getting a glimpse into his mind with as much skill as when a teenage boy yanks a pair of panties off a girl. Since he can't have his way with Will Graham's mind, Hannibal wants, he claims, for him to at least understand that the difference between swallowing another's heart and entering the core of his being is miniscule; what he wants Graham to understand is that it's the fact of having someone else inside you—whether it be his flesh or his point of view—that really matters.

The sun is now coming in through the window and I close the book. I manage to sleep for a few hours, enough to dream that I am in a hospital bed that is identical to the one I am sleeping in, and that the bed is in a long rectangular room, painted white and filled with a light that enters through a row of enormous windows. Someone wearing white coveralls slowly approaches my bed—all the others, lined up to my left and my right, are empty—with both hands clasped behind his back, as if overacting the role of inspector. It's Hannibal, who comes right up to my ear and says: *Caliban has a good claim to Patagonian ancestry.* With those words he exhales a vapor that permeates my brain. Then he remains standing next to the head of the bed, like a guard who has not been given orders to leave. The combination of white and light blinds me and the vapor that fills all the cavities in my skull leaves me in a daze. *Caliban has a good claim to Patagonian ancestry.* I look at the bed next to me, where the voice is now coming from, and I see that it is not empty, as I had thought: in it is an emaciated man with scraggly blond hair. It's Bruce Chatwin, or Chatwin's ghost, eyes half closed and talking nonstop, in a monotone but with urgency, about how Shakespeare was inspired by a Patagonian Indian to create Caliban in *The Tempest*, he says; and that Shakespeare read Pigafetta, the first chronicler of Patagonia, and that's where he got the monster Caliban; and that he can prove it, he says, and he starts down the list: both monsters rant and rave, crying out for the god Setebos; both are semi-human; both learn a foreign language; both contain the fury and impotence of the New World; and both conceal some kind of threat against the civilized world, the incomprehensible babble of a civilization that is rotting around the edges. *Chat, chat, Chatwin,* I think in my bed. Who coined that phrase? The Chatwinian whispering continues, always in a monotone. Chatwin, who set about to recount his own death, the consequence of mushrooms he ate in China. Chatwin and the various versions, that he actually might have contracted AIDS in Patagonia. *Chat, chat, Chatwin.* Caliban, cannibal, Hannibal. Each place produces its own monsters, and I don't see where in Patagonia Shakespeare's exorbitant monster or the well-dressed monster with such good manners who will not leave my bedside might fit. Chatwin keeps chatting, and he points out that I must not forget that in the last novel of the saga, Hannibal escapes with Detective Sterling to Buenos Aires, and I also must not forget how much his book, Chatwin's book, contributed to the situation in which no foreigner who visits Buenos Aires fails to take a short trip to Patagonia, as well. Chatwin, then, is the one who imported Caliban and Hannibal to Patagonia: it must have been very far-flung and tedious for him to dig into the monsters of indigenous mythologies. Chatwin's interminable monologue contrasts with the silence of Hannibal, who again leans over me. This time he brushes right against my ear to talk to me, which makes me shiver with culpability: I am just like he is, he tells me. That what I'm doing—sticking my nose into the lives, the stories, and the minds of other people—is the same as what he does. That what I call a two-voiced narrative is in fact cannibalism. I awake, haunted and with a headache.

SIX

Susana, fat as a cow, welcomed me into all those houses where luxury is displayed and harmony sustained by the possession of a television set. Wandering around these two mesetas—El Cuy and Somuncurá—I've heard stories about people who lost their parents when they were babies and were immediately yanked away from the place of their birth and taken to live elsewhere under conditions of covert slavery; stories about eight-year-old children who ride fifteen kilometers on puny bicycles to get to a rural school, their snot dripping down to their chins; stories about little girls whose parents, tired of the uncle raping them, wanted to trade them for a herd of goats. I've heard all of these stories in houses with Susana Giménez, one of our biggest TV personalities, on in the background, a Susana who is forever sexier and more hilarious, wrapped in furs and with the Perito Moreno Glacier behind her, as if to assert that only a colossus of nature can possibly act as the bodyguard to a national myth. Susana Giménez, without a doubt, is in Patagonia: at the glacier, which is visited by statesmen and tourists who spend foreign currency, and also in El Cuy, which is visited by almost no one who spends currency of any kind.

And, on the ubiquitous TV, is also Tinelli, with his pseudo-hippie locks, and Ranni on the Retro Channel, and the countless talking heads who believe that seriousness about your work should be accompanied by seriously overacted facial expressions, and, of course, soccer games. They say that once, about ten years ago, there was nothing on but a porno flick. As it happens, everybody in El Cuy is forced to watch the same channel: since nobody can afford to pay for cable TV individually, the development association subscribes to Direct TV and is responsible—through some kind of device or something that sounded to me like a science fiction plot from the seventies—for transmitting the signal to all the television sets in town. So the people in charge of deciding what the whole town watches on any given day are the development commissioner, his children, or someone in their orbit. If they decide on Susana, it's Susana; if they decide on the comedy show "Polémica en el bar," it's "Polémica en el bar." Sometimes a local will come to them with a suggestion, but it seems the commissioner and his orbit are impervious to all suggestions. They say that one night the commissioner or someone in his orbit got distracted and left the entire town at the mercy of a porno flick. The local women went to bang their fists on the metal door. In the backyard of the house of the commissioner's sister, who is also his neighbor and his secretary, the turkeys were desperately clucking away and the ñandúes were running around in circles, terrified. One of the thirty people who figure in the El Cuy telephone book even called him on the telephone, because here the telephone is used only in cases of emergency.

• • •

The commissioner talks to me, if by that we understand a babbling monotone, and watches TV at the same time. His wife and children are also watching TV. One of his sons just returned from Junín de los Andes. He had gone there to study at the technical school, to become an agronomy technician, but he came back before completing his degree. Everybody in this house has flabby cheeks and is slightly slack-jawed, as if, from the very first day the screen appeared before their eyes, they had remained frozen in that expression forever.

• • •

The father of this development commissioner, who in turn was the former development commissioner, says that the problem is that kids these days don't even know how to ride a horse. They have no idea what it's like out in the country. They go to school, where they're taught who knows what, and then, thanks to that, they can't work in the country or go to the university. A few drag themselves to Maquinchao to finish high school or to the technical school in Junín. So here they are, hanging out on street corners, of no use to anybody. In limbo. He, on the other hand, made sure to take his son with him to their land, ever since he was little, at least twice a week. So he'd know what it was like, even though he raised him here in El Cuy. And to think that now, even so, he has to take care of the land almost alone: at his age and alone. Peons are an expense that he can ill afford. Before, when sons worked the land, the family could keep goats, sheep. They could remain together. Now everything's a mess, meaningless. And now he, who built everything himself, has to deal with everything himself. That must be some people's fate. By the time he was eight, his father had abandoned them and his mother had died. From one day to the next he never saw his two sisters again, and somehow he had to survive, working as a peon. From there he became a foreman, then a manager, and then a *mediero*, meaning he shared the expenses and the profits with the owner of the land he worked on for more than thirty years, then the development commissioner, and then he returned to the country, now as a landowner. And to think that when he got there he didn't even speak *castilla*, Spanish, he says, only *la lengua*, the tongue. That's how, for short, the descendents of the Mapuches call *la lengua mapu dungun*, more commonly known as Mapuche. That was before; now they no longer speak it. Or only every very once in a while; if he meets up with one of his sisters, for example. He found one of them again, the one who wasn't more than a few months old when they moved them off the land, just a few years ago. At the bus station in Bahía Blanca. No, it wasn't by accident: he found her through the police superintendent there, in El Cuy, who was a friend of his. They'd already been friends for years before that conversation came up, the one that led to that encounter at the bus station. The superintendent would always come over: they'd drink maté, have a barbecue, an *asado*. They'd talk about the country, the harvest, things going on around town. Why should they talk about family? The kids would be hanging around and his wife would be doing her thing, that was enough. What's there to say about it, anyway? One night, talking about neighbors and other people, he doesn't know what exactly, the subject of a nurse the superintendent knew came up. From there, from Bahía, where the superintendent was from. She'd kept her last name, and that's how, on a night that seemed the same as all other nights, he discovered, after fifty years, what had become of his little sister. He went to the station in Bahía with his other sister, because he'd always kept in touch with her. That day at the station was something else. He and his sister poked each other with their elbows: could that be her, maybe that one. When they realized who it was, neither of them knew what to do or say. Including and most of all that sister: she had just found out a week ago not only that she had two siblings there in Río Negro but that she was adopted. How pretty she looked at the station, with her matching suit. With her, every once in a while, when they see each other, they speak the language.

Right now they say, speak the tongue, I dunno . . . but why am I gonna talk to people when they don't understand it, that's what I think . . . why am I gonna talk if nobody knows what I'm sayin' . . . so, then . . . The other day it happened . . . somethin' happened. Out in the country, two trucks arrived with North Americans, lookin' for mines . . . They wanted to explain something to me, but I didn't know what they was sayin' . . . and I wanted to 'cause the language is kinda alike . . . kinda . . . I felt like trippin' them up with the language and givin' it to 'em and they'd give it to me, but they ain't gonna understand. So . . . well, one shows up who seems like I could understand somethin' . . . Yeah, I understood him a little because we were used to it with a nun who always came here, a North American one, and she talked pretty clear, a sister of the church who came here a lot to the house, spent days and days in the country,

made friends with the girls, made . . . She was good
because she went around and proselytized around . . .
but I didn't understand nothin' they said . . . no way,
no I felt like comin' out and speakin' the language to
them . . .

Statement by the father of the development commissioner,
published in the book El Cuy. Una vasta soledad,
[El Cuy: A Vast Solitude] *edited by Freddy Masera.*

I cross Route 6, which divides the town in two and is the only
paved road in El Cuy, and walk to the only hostel in El Cuy,
where I am the only guest. Goyo, the proprietor, is also watching TV. Annexed to his hostel is a store that sells mandarin
oranges and nail polish, a small shop where his wife sells "gift
items" she brings from General Roca, and this bar where Goyo
watches TV while his only customer struggles against the alcohol level in his blood the way one confronts the Devil. Goyo
was among the first to settle in this town, and he doesn't need
more than one eye to see everything there is to see. In this way
he makes it clear that he might be one-eyed but he's nobody's
fool. When I arrive, he leaves the boxing match on TV, his
glass of Fernet on the table, and makes his way to the grocery
store to sell me a few things that have occurred to me to buy
at that moment. Nothing will break this thermos, he assures
me, and he slaps it down on the floor. Then he picks it up and
tells me that I can go into the kitchen to make myself some tea,
that I can take anything there I want but I should stop spoiling
the dog. From the window of the store I see a woman walk by
with a firm stride, accompanied by a girl whose hair has been
brushed as if her head were a sports field: a straight white line

divides two sections where barrettes placed with perfect symmetry hold the hair that has been previously raked with a wet comb. Or, as if it were the board for a table game I'd never seen, laid out neatly, awaiting only the arrival of the players. When I walk through the bar to reach the kitchen, I see that the two of them are bawling out the man who, despite their vigorous insistence, cannot get himself out of the chair. And even though he can barely speak, he manages to ask me, with pronunciation that shows how uncomfortable at times it is for him to have a tongue inside his own mouth:

"Are you one of those seminarians who's always hanging around here?"

Through one of those strange convergences that sometimes happens in life, the three credos that wield influence over the town and its surrounding area come together in Milka: the Evangelicals, who are constantly sending out pastors to spread their message; Catholicism, which does what it can; and El Maruchito, the boy who was brutally murdered in a nearby hamlet at the beginning of the century and has, through popular belief, been consecrated as a saint. Milka, as can be expected, has her supporters and her detractors. When I arrive at her house for an interview, she offers me a seat, and the first thing she tells me, before I settle in, is that I probably want a 7 Up because every day everybody is probably offering me maté and my stomach must be at the bursting point. It's going to be difficult, I think—after drinking so much maté that I've been reminded of when I was ten years old and my stomach almost burst from an ulcer—for anyone to convince me that Milka doesn't have her powers.

...

In the living room of her house, the TV is on but the sound is off. Milka tells me that the idea for the Milikilin Huitral Workshop, which she set up and still runs, started as an initiative of the Catholic Church. She says that at the end of the eighties, a priest came to see her and told her that in the face of the schism—forgive the hyperbole—that was occurring in town between Catholics and Evangelicals, it would be important to unite the women in the community—women of Mapuche origin, excluded from the labor force—in a shared activity: to recover the textile crafts of their ancestors and to which a dose of religious teachings could be added, with a Catholic stamp, of course. This sort of catechism sui generis would be—the priest told her and that's how it turned out—in the hands of Milka, who until then had tended the shop in the front of her house: a combination grocery store and boutique, which everybody agreed was the most sophisticated shop in town. She agreed. Basically, she was drawn to the idea of spinning: it was something she'd learned from her aunt and done as a child, without her parents knowing. Spinning was only for Indians. The idea of a spinning workshop became Milka's room of her own: it would make legitimate what she had done previously in hiding, clandestinely. And not only that. She would also be disseminating it. Milka told the priest, yes, she would be in charge of the catechism, and inside she was thinking that, above all, she would be in charge of getting the women out of their houses, teaching them how to earn a living and how to stand up to their husbands, how to be able to come and go as they wished. And to think, as a child she didn't feel like even lifting her eyes off the ground when people spoke to her, she said.

It wasn't easy, because of the men who were against it, because of the women who were afraid, and because materials were scarce. However, the crisis had hit everybody around there so strongly—mostly peons or owners of barely one hundred, two hundred sheep, and at the end of the eighties, wool was worth nothing—that the husbands backed off, and a few women could meet three times a week and recover—in the majority of cases, learn for the first time—the skills of spinning, dying, and working a loom. At first, when they had nothing, she taught them to weave, using yarn they'd unwind from old sweaters. Milka would weave in the yarns and tell them that the same thing that had bent the backs of their mothers and grandmothers out in the countryside could now be their way to support themselves, make money to help at home. Many gave up. Sometimes it's not easy to go back to doing what your grandmothers did. Or maybe not, she doesn't really believe that's it. Rather it's apathy, a kind of autism that takes hold of them. When they get like that, she loses her patience with them.

Everything is made by hand here: the wool, the dyes, even your brains are made by hand! she shouts at them when she sees them be so subservient, so out of it. But that only happens every once in a while. But always, without fail, she tells them that there is only one God.

Milka never instilled in them scorn for or resentment of their husbands or any thirst for liberation. How could she, anyway, when the numbers don't add up. You've got to plan things in life: know your limitations and your strengths. She always knew how to do that. How to take life by the horns; when there's sorrow, you keep quiet and carry on. Milka has a colorful scarf covering her head and her curlers—tonight she and the association folks are putting on their annual Bingo game to raise money to pay for all the extra expenses of the workshop—and not even all those things piled on her head can soften the toughness in her face or nudge it toward the ridiculous. An emaciated woman and two little girls come in. The woman is her mother, Milka says, who forced her to marry her first boyfriend when she was fifteen. The same man who is still her husband. Because of "what they would say," she didn't have a chance to find anything out about the boy, and now they've spent more than twenty years together. Her mother looks on from the other side of the table and nods with an absent half-smile. She is completely deaf and is already dressed for Bingo tonight, wearing a double-loop necklace that doesn't look anything like what her obviously indigenous ancestors wore. The two girls whisper, change the channel, and turn up the volume on the TV.

Today there are twenty-three women who have stable work, Milka raises her voice and continues, and the workshop is run as a nonprofit organization. A few years ago, when they were able to start using natural dyes, an ancestral technique that was almost lost, they received a grant from Proinder, the Small Farmer Development Project of the Argentine Ministry of Agriculture. The people from the Catholic Church, who were the first to push the project, tell her that this seems more and more like a business than a catechizing mission. It's a venture, Milka remarks, it's an act of consciousness-raising that these women need. It's not about liberation or about revelation or any of that mumbo-jumbo: when she says consciousness-raising she means making it possible for these women to be able to think for themselves, acknowledge their Mapuche origins, speak up if there's something they don't like, give their opinions, take some initiative. Milka shows me a legal-sized binder where she keeps an account of the history of the workshop, testimonials, newspaper articles. She assembled the binder, she tells me, last year, when she thought that she would die from the aneurysm they had to remove from her head and that all of this would simply fall apart. She shows me a diagram she created, she says, so that the women can learn to bring up an issue and discuss it, so they can develop skills for expressing themselves, responding. In that binder, she keeps a record of what happens month to month, the responses she receives, and the mindset every member of the workshop needs in order to get ahead:

Monthly plan of tasks/conflicts/issues to resolve

1) Problem or Issue	There aren't enough handicrafts
2) Why?	Not enough yarn
	Not enough dye
	Not enough desire to work
	We don't charge
	The sacrifice isn't worth it
3) Mindset	Maria: Talk about things head on

Luisa: Overcome apathy
Nora: Be more disciplined
Antonia: Keep quiet to avoid problems

(Simultaneously, a short and pleasant-looking woman enters through the door on the left, and through the door on the right, the outside door, enters a man of about forty with a cheerful expression on his face. The woman sits down in an armchair to the left of the table where Milka and I are talking. The man says hello and keeps walking, followed by another man. They sit at a table farther away and disappear behind one of those fake wood sliding doors that look like accordions.)

He's always been like that, doing lots of things at once, says the woman who settled into the armchair. As a child, he was already like that. You had to go looking for him in the trees, at the bottom of wells, waiting for him to return at midnight on an exhausted horse. Must be because of all the energy left for him by his three older brothers, her three older sons, who all died as children. The woman takes advantage of Milka talking to one of the girls to tell me this. It is, it seems, her way of introducing herself as a mother. When I ask her about the other three, the dead boys, she answers as if she were talking about the lambs that died this spring because it didn't rain the whole winter and they didn't have enough grass to eat. There's something cheerful in her gaze, as if she never spent an ounce of energy questioning the laws of nature. I look at them both, the two mothers, Fabián's and Milka's. One is stretched out in the armchair, talking whenever she has a chance, and the other is sitting up stiffly in her chair, impervious to what is being said around her thanks to a couple of eardrums in a sorry state, sitting up straight so that her blue dress and the double-loop necklace will still be in place five hours later, when the Bingo and dancing start. Although Milka didn't make it clear to me before, it wasn't difficult to deduce which one made the demand for the early marriage.

Milka tells me that the man who came in with her husband is a wholesaler and distributor, and they regularly sell their wool to him. With his two or three thousand sheep, Fabián is a land-owner of sorts in these central mesetas of Río Negro. I don't think that things there, behind the panel, are excessively simple for the wool buyer. Fabián started out selling clothes he would purchase in Roca and carry in a bag from town to town. Hitch-hiking, because he didn't even own a car. And you'd have to see the kind of towns, says Fabián, who has already said good-bye to the buyer with a smile reserved for old friends. Now he saves all that roaming around for going back and forth to the country, where he lives half the time, and for his annual *cami-nata*, or trek, to El Maruchito. For seven years now he's gone every October; would have been eight if he hadn't been in the hospital in Buenos Aires this last October because of Milka's aneurysm.

• • •

La ermita de Maruchito, Maruchito's Shrine, is about fifty kilome-ters from El Cuy, surrounded by open meseta and announced by a sign that says, "Miracle Worker of the Patagonia Meseta." Next to the shrine there is a wooden cart and in the driver's seat is a plastic doll standing tall, staring out at the desert. I look at that doll's eyes and consider that we have spent our childhoods sleeping in dark rooms under the watchful gaze of who knows how many of those staring, static, untiring eyes. At one point in my childhood, I remember, they scared me so much that I slept with all my dolls in my bed, tangled up in my legs, trying to prevent any of their eyes from crossing with my own sleepless ones. It never bothered me to sleep with the enemy. We were about thirty dolls and me, and we could barely fit in the bed. I used to say that I took the trouble to tuck them in every night because I loved them, but the truth is, I was terrified.

A doll with those same eyes, in the seat of this cart that doesn't go anywhere along a desert road, sits in for the child who gave rise to the legend of Maruchito. Pedro Frías was his name, and he worked as a *marucho*, or peon, who accompanied the caravans of peddlers carrying wool, guanaco skins, ostrich feathers, and certain edibles from deep inside Patagonia to a city or port. Among the various versions that are told about his death is the one Elías Chucair tells, that one night in the summer of 1916, the caravan Pedro Frías was traveling with stopped at a spot on the meseta of Cuy, between the hamlets of Aguada Guzmán and Cerro Policía, the site of the current shrine. While they made a fire for the maté de rigueur, the *marucho* felt like disobeying the foreman's rules and grabbed the guitar that was leaning against a wheel. He started to play, and though he'd never in his life played either this or any other instrument, something seemed to be guiding his fingers. He played melodious, compelling chords. Everybody else kept doing their chores, getting ready for a little rest before the sun went down, grateful because for once they had some background music, and there was Maruchito, playing the guitar as if it was the only thing he'd ever done since the day he was born. Gracefully, as if he knew just what he was doing. Which, apparently, infuriated the foreman, who stabbed him twice in the stomach, killing him. Maruchito didn't die right away, though; it was worse than that. The poor boy bled to death slowly in the house of a curandera, a local healer, whom they passed on their way. The legend of Maruchito was started by his own murderer. It seems that shortly after this event, the foreman went crazy, abandoned his family and everything he had, and spent the rest of his life wandering alone throughout the country, beset by terror. Based on what happened to him, it was believed that Maruchito kept watch over the entire meseta from wherever he happened to be, and that each day he could punish whoever deserved to be punished and help the good souls who needed him. The large number of offerings at the shrine testify to this: plaques with expressions of gratitude covering a vast array of subjects / plastic and natural flowers / photographs of people hugging at a party, a wedding, a birth / miniature guitars / car or truck license plates / a baseball hat / a racing pennant / an image of the Virgin Mary holding Jesus in her arms / three rosaries / more dolls / a milonga signed by Horacio Vargas that reads:

On the road before dawn, we greet the new day / Behind us, Cerro Policía, then we continue on our way / Atop my black horse, riding slowly, riding free / I

ask myself again, who this Maruchito might be / They
promise him the world for the miracles he makes / We
took this long journey to see you, little saint / Maruchito, Maruchito, king of the valley and the road so far
/ A dream cut short, a child who played the guitar /
Maruchito, Maruchito, king of the valley and the road
so far / A dream cut short by a killer in a cart.

So much for testimonials to his providential spirit. Other events
bear witness to the fact that his vengeful spirit has remained active ever since he first took revenge on his foreman. Only that
now, the equation it uses has morphed into the exact opposite:
instead of forcing those who offend him to wander lost around
the byways, he stands in their way and forces them to stop.
Soon after I arrived in the area, several people assured me that
whoever passes by his shrine without stopping and making
an offering will be condemned to suffer some kind of mishap
along their way. In El Cuy, in Aguada Guzmán, and in all the
hamlets in the surrounding areas, there's not a soul who won't
confirm this. Elías Chucair tells the story of a journalist and a
photographer from Buenos Aires who came to visit him at his
home in Jacobacci one afternoon, stunned by what had just
happened to them. They were on their way somewhere else,
but since they knew Chucair from before, they took a detour
to see if he could clear up a few things for them. They drove
from Buenos Aires in a car that had been working perfectly
till then, they told him, but along the road, about 130 or 150
kilometers from Jacobacci, the front wheel fell off and they lost
control. They were still trying to figure out what could have

caused it, looking at each other to confirm that they were still alive, when a man on horseback rode up to them. He listened to everything they had to tell him and then he asked them if they'd stopped there.

"There where?"

"There, at Maruchito's."

He pointed to the *ermita* with his riding crop, then explained to them that it happened because over there, about two hundred meters away, was Maruchito's shrine, and everybody who passes it without stopping ends up having some kind of accident. And he started telling them all the other incidents likes theirs that he knew about. He talked and pointed with his crop without ever getting off his horse, like Aballay in Antonio Di Benedetto's story. Might that gaucho be emulating the hermits who never descend from their mountains so they can remain closer to God? Might he also be haunted by some culpability? Might he be the ghost of the foreman?

Although the shrine indicates that Maruchito is praised only for his good deeds, I think that the faithful might revere most deeply his capacity for underlying revenge, his ability to exact due punishment. After all, most of them are descendents of a people that was decimated and has had to learn to survive in a culture in which revenge is viewed, based not only on the religious discourse but also on its endless secular variants, as something negative and punishable by law. Most likely, however, it is not ancestral vindication that nourishes the desire for revenge but the lack of basic rights as citizens of this country, which most of the faithful of the guitar-playing doll experience:

a flashpoint Maruchito's cold eyes secretly indicate while he distracts all of us with his parodies of revenge along the road.

• • •

Fabián tells me that several years ago, in El Cuy, there was a Catholic priest named Marcelino, who, though a pretty good friend of his, always made fun of his pilgrimage to Maruchito. One day, Marcelino drove past the shrine, and a few minutes later his truck stopped. There was no way to get it started. After more than an hour of checking everything and touching all the various cables in the engine, which seemed to him the most unfathomable of all mysteries, he got back into his truck, freezing to death, and, with the choke on and the gas pedal to the floor, he vowed to organize a pilgrimage to the so-called saint if he got out alive. When the truck finally started, he took it upon himself to organize a rapprochement between the Catholic Church and Maruchito's followers, which is on display every October. During the annual pilgrimage, when the ceremony is performed in front of the shrine, the Catholic priests say that in Maruchito we must see the children in all the nearby hamlets who live "in abusive situations, without medical attention, without the love of their parents." In the video Fabián shot, which we are watching on the television set we managed to wrestle away from the girls, the priest calls all those children "our Maruchitos."

In the same video, the priests are giving speeches next to the cart driven by the doll who looks out at the desert. The Evangelicals, who have known how to capitalize on their activities

and gain a lot of ground against the Catholics, have no role
here. For them Maruchito is dead, a pastor of one of the three
congregations operating in El Cuy told me one day, and they
have no tradition of worshiping the dead, only God, who is
alive and watches over them. For a similar reason, local Evangelicals don't want to dig into their ancestry, into their indigenous roots. That would be like returning to the past, to the
dead, to a time when their people were decimated, annihilated.
Those gods didn't protect our Mapuche ancestors very much,
it seems, according to the pastor, who must be about forty
years old and was raised as a Catholic. Even her father didn't
want anything to do with the cults of the past, all that stuff that
today some people—especially people from the city, who don't
suffer and don't see what people suffer here—want to reclaim
in some great re-encounter with their roots and who knows
what else. For her and the members of her church, who are
practically all descendents of Mapuches, there is one very clear
God, who is not going to abandon them this time around.

The video continues; the girls remain quiet and watch, and
I think that for the first time I am watching something on a
television set in El Cuy that interests me. And drinking 7 Up.
Fabián shot this video during the pilgrimage he made in 2002.
No, he wouldn't call it a pilgrimage; he prefers *caminata*. That's
what it is for him, a trek. Not in the sense of an athletic activity, but in some other sense that he doesn't know how to
define. But he can offer some details: it's something that he
does alone and for himself, something that will not bring any
concrete benefits to him or his family, something that struck
him one day, just like that, like a touch of madness. Tomorrow,

I'm going to walk to Maruchito, he said, and he left. And since then, every year he does the same thing: he walks into the open country, and keeps going for more or less fifteen hours, until he gets to the shrine. And he does all that just because. Because that's what he likes to do. The solitude, the sensation of being all alone out there in the country, to think things over, to make plans. It's not like he means to: things just pop into his head on their own, and it's as if they find places to settle in with each step he takes, effortlessly, without that feeling of them going round and round without getting anywhere, like what happens when he sets his mind to solving a problem. Everything happens on its own, smoothly, without any effort. He carries on conversations: he gets into fights with one of his peons who hasn't been working well lately, with his kids who don't obey him, with Milka, of course, he fights and then they make up. All of it happens out there, along the way. How strange, he doesn't even remember how he got the touch of madness the first time. And then it turned into something more urgent, into storms and blows of madness. This last October was the only time he didn't go, because of what happened with Milka. Even though she told him, go, go, she'd be well taken care of there at that hospital in Buenos Aires, with all the doctors and nurses. Their son went instead. He took exactly the same route, going straight through the country from El Cuy to Bajada Colorada, where Maruchito is. He did it for his father and now it turns out that he, his son, has also been bitten by the bug.

And Milka, what does she think? That everybody believes in what they can believe in.

It's not so much a question of believing in Maruchito, Fabián explains to me, because the truth is, he wouldn't visit Maruchito if it was a matter of going by car. He wouldn't feel it, it would seem fake to him. It's that trek that matters. For example, he doesn't pray and never did. Even now he doesn't pray or ask for anything, but he does have to admit that at difficult moments, like when Milka was sick, Maruchito appears to him. Not from the sky, with a halo, like in the movies; no, he sees concrete images. For example, he opened an account book, and there was the leaflet they'd given him at the last meeting in October. Or, he was looking for a receipt book and found an image of Marucho. It's more like Maruchito comes to him when he knows that things are tough. It's a little like that. It's as if Maruchito was also happy about that trek he takes through the country; maybe the first time it wasn't a touch of madness but more like a summons, who knows. In that respect, things escape him, he wouldn't know how to define it or how to take communion like the people he sees there in October, more and more of them all the time. Honestly, he goes just because.

I have met with but one or two persons in the course of my life who understood the art of Walking, that is, of taking walks—who had a genius, so to speak, for *sauntering*, which word is beautifully derived "from idle people who roved about the country, in the Middle Ages, and asked charity, under pretense of going *a la Sainte-Terre*," to the Holy Land, till the children exclaimed, "There goes a *Sainte-Terrer*," a Saunterer, a Holy-Lander . . . Some, however, would derive the word from *sans terre* without land or a home, which, therefore, in the good sense, will mean, having no particular home, but equally at home everywhere. For this is the secret of successful sauntering . . . It is true, we are but faint-hearted crusaders, even the walkers, nowadays, who undertake no persevering, never-ending enterprises. Our expeditions are but tours, and come round again at evening to the old hearthside from which we set out. Half the walk is but retracing our steps. We should go forth on the shortest walk, perchance, in the spirit of undying adventure, never to return, prepared to send back our embalmed hearts only as relics to our desolate kingdoms.

Walking, *Henry David Thoreau, 1862*

He's always been like that, since he was little, says his mother from the armchair.

In that video, where Fabián filmed the gathering of the faithful at the shrine and the priests' speeches, he also filmed his own trek. Minutes and more minutes of the meseta where a pillar of rocks appears out of the blue, or there's a foreground of ice plants. Sometimes, even more unexpected than the rocks, he himself makes an appearance. He'd place the camera on a higher spot, walk a few steps back, and film himself, he explains to me. There are also interior scenes: a room in an adobe house where Fabián sleeps on the floor in his sleeping bag. It's a lean-to about six hours from El Cuy, which he always calculates he'll reach to spend the night and then keep walking the next day, early in the morning. Like those houses along the

Camino de Santiago, which are open the whole month of the pilgrimage, ready to give food and drink to whoever arrives, except here Fabián is the only pilgrim. Trekker, he corrects me. He wants to fast forward, but I tell him not to, I want to see everything in detail, though, truth is, what really interests me is to sit there in front of the screen, completely immersed in this Big Brother being shown for me alone, while time passes, the girls also watch, Milka offers me more 7 Up, the mothers grow quiet, time passes, and I watch TV, too. I gorge myself on TV while outside, every once in a while, a truck drives fast down the road that splits El Cuy in two.

• • •

There lived here in Río Negro Province another character whose virtuosity on the guitar also could never be fully explained. Bernabé Lucero was his name, and he lived in a place everybody passes but nobody inhabits: Bajo del Gualicho, on the far eastern edge of the province. Bernabé Lucero was illiterate, he lived in a cave, and he ate whatever he could find. Bernabé was evasive and enigmatic, but even so, three things about him were well known: he very much liked to be alone, he very much liked red wine, and he played the guitar divinely. Whenever he played in bars in the towns, he left everyone awestruck. His father was mestizo and his mother was pure Tehuelche. One of Lucero's brothers on his father's side, who is about eighty today, says that sometimes he would spend some time in Valcheta, where he lives, and then he would sleep in a kind of shed he has out back. He'd come and stay there, and

sometimes he'd disappear and nobody would be able to figure
out where he'd gone. He knew that for sure, the half brother
says: there were nights when he'd return late from a neighbor's
house, where he used to go to play cards, and he'd shine the
flashlight into the shed to see if Bernabé was around, and he
wouldn't find him even if he turned the last burlap sack inside
out. The next day, while they were drinking maté, he'd ask him
where he'd been the night before, and he'd say, sleeping in the
shed, where else would he be. It was strange, very strange. He
wouldn't explain anything. And much less when he'd ask him
how he learned to play the guitar. Not a peep. Until one night
he found him a little more in his cups than usual. Then he did
like to talk. And then he told him about his mother, the Tehuelche, and the time she took him to Conesa. Bernabé must
have been about twelve, he thought, and on that trip he heard
a man play the guitar for the first time. It was in a little hotel
where they were staying or in the house of some family friends,
his half brother doesn't remember exactly. What he does remember is that Bernabé insisted that since then, he couldn't
think of anything else. The guitar chords produced a feeling
and a desire to live that he'd never felt before. Since that night,
he told him, that guitarist started to appear in his dreams. Until
one night the guitarist told him that if he wanted to play like
him he had to go to the Gualicho Cave. If you're brave, you'll
come out playing the guitar, he told him; if not, you'll go crazy.
Everybody from around there knows that what he was telling
him to do wasn't simple, because since they were kids they'd
heard about that place, about the cave. His own father would
tell him that it was next to a road that the Indians had made

many years before, and that whenever he passed by there he'd leave something—a coin, a cigarette—so he wouldn't get lost when he returned and to prevent anything bad from happening to him along the way. Because many had gotten lost and started to wander around in circles until they died of thirst, hunger, exhaustion, or anger. But, according to what Bernabé told him that night when his tongue had loosened up, he didn't have any fear or any doubt. He did what the man in his dreams told him to do: he entered that cave where they say the Devil lives. And there, so it seems, he had to pass several tests: first, a nest of vipers, and then some bulls who were fighting each other to the death and who you have to know how to get past at precisely the right moment when they pull back to gather their momentum and go at it again, and likewise, several other tests. And, as it seems like he dealt with all of it, he also did well with the guitar. There were times when Bernabé would come back disheveled and say that he'd been wrestling with the Devil in the forest, that he'd appeared to him in the shape of a bull. Other times, he'd slowly start to prepare himself to play something calmly, something intimate, you might call it, and Bernabé would tell him that that night his guitar was going to play divinely, as if all on its own, because his Friend was coming to play with him. That is, sometimes he didn't get along with the Devil but other times they were friends. A little like what happens to us with everybody.

> Lucero was peculiar, he didn't like to be asked for music . . . he played what he felt like, or rather if they said to him "Don Bernabé, why don't you play a milonga" . . . ah, he wouldn't even hear, he'd come out with a

ranchera . . . he didn't like anybody to bother him . . .
he was deeply . . . as if possessed by the guitar . . . that's
what I always noticed.

Testimony of Floriano López in El Bajo del Gualicho,
edited by Freddy Masera.

That night I leave El Cuy. I take one of those buses that have
forced me, throughout the region, to get up in the middle of
the night or arrive in a deserted town at four in the morning,
because they're the only ones that run—with any luck. In the
seat next to me sits a masculine-looking woman who says she's
a missionary and asks me a question. I answer in a monosyl-
lable and bury myself in the darkness that appears on the other
side of the glass when I open the curtain stiffened by the dust
that blows in through the cracks. At exactly ten minutes to
four in the morning the bus stops. It simply stops. The driver
looks over everything and recounts the mechanical problems
he finds, as if he were announcing a soccer game, in detail and
with excitement. He waits, I think, for somebody to react, for
somebody to say something, give some suggestions, or speak a
word of encouragement or even of discouragement. How cold
it is, and it's November. Maybe it's the belt. He'll have to check
the radiator. But nobody says anything. The driver gets on and
off, mumbling something about a hose that he doesn't have or
he does have but it's shorter or longer that what he needs. He
leaves the door open and more cold air comes in. I close my
eyes, hoping I can make all this nuisance around me disappear.
I employ the strategy of the ostrich to deal with this: I, too, have
the excuse of being a native. Or should I say the strategy of the

ñandú? In the seat in front of me, I hear the whisperings of a couple who boarded at a hamlet a few kilometers before this unplanned stop: a scrawny man with his hat perched uneasily on a mat of smooth hair, and a sturdy woman, much younger than he, with weather-beaten cheeks. They seemed exuberant when they got on, as if excited at the idea of finally getting out of there, and very affectionate: he kissed her constantly with a kind of childish candor, as if he were a grateful little boy who, after years, meets up again with his mother and discovers that she is just like she was when he was young, unscathed by time. Then something crosses my mind: after having spent days in El Cuy, walking around everywhere, this is the first time I've gotten into or onto anything with wheels. I come out of my forced passivity and ask the couple in front of me something about Maruchito. He's about to answer but she tells me to keep my nose out of other people's business. She's really angry. The missionary tells me that even though she's Catholic, she's heard about what I'm asking.

But why is it any of her business! I hear from the seat in front of me.

And you don't go around talking like that to people you don't know. He doesn't answer, or at least I don't hear him. The thing is, the missionary says, locals here claim that not only do you have to stop in front of Maruchito: you have to stop and leave something for him. Something like a flower, a candle, a handkerchief, anything, but something. Ah, so you have to leave something for him, as well. I sink into my seat, close my eyes again, and the eyes of the doll in that cart appear in front of me. Those glassy eyes, staring out at the desert. I can't think of Maruchito in the guise of a suffering peon; I see him precisely as that doll that now, in the darkness, must have a half smile on his lips, thinking about what is happening to me because I didn't leave something for him. A kind of Chucky, the evil doll. Standing in his carriage, seemingly inanimate but in reality on high alert, waiting for the moment when one human will pay for all the scum of the species he or she belongs to. Or, I also see him, throughout this long night stranded out on the road, like a saint with backbone, one who's not willing to turn the other cheek. No new testament or new reconciliation or new politically correct practices: let's get back to that eye for an eye, which we never should have given up in the first place.

SEVEN

Evita, Gardel, Kirchner, Ginóbili, Pérez Esquivel, Favaloro, Fangio, Borges, Maradona, Coria, Sábato. On the poster, little headshots of them all surround the central image of Sarmiento and his famous sentence: *"Hombre, Pueblo, Nación, Estado, todo: todo está en los humildes bancos de esta escuela."* "Man, People, Nation, State, everything: everything sits on the humble desks of this school." The poster, which clearly was designed to be printed in bright colors though the budget could pay only for that faded yellow, is hanging on the door of the school where I'm staying. In El Caín, the only town on the mythical Meseta de Somuncurá, there are no lodgings, but the school lets me use one of the bunk beds in the rooms where the female students sleep, and, once they all leave for the day, the office bathroom to shower. While I'm showering, the voices of the girls and boys, who at that hour are playing soccer in the open field out back, filter through the window. There's something voyeuristic about being in a school when everybody has left, as if public spaces can only be visited when the public is around. Traces of the day's lessons remain on the blackboards, and of the day's meals on the floor, and none of that includes me in the slightest: I feel a little like a detective who visits a crime scene, though in this case I can't be expected to solve anything. On one of those afternoons, during my shower, I realized that I wasn't hearing any sounds at all. The children must have changed schedules, I thought at first, but I quickly remembered that schools are no longer what they used to be. What if everybody was dead, and waiting for me in one of those classrooms was one of those teenage mass shooters who decides to bring to school the gun that their parents keep in the bedside table along with their glasses and aspirin? All these empty classrooms and there I was in the shower, where something always happens to women in movies. I stepped out of the shower with suds in my hair and locked the door to the office. The silence persisted and suddenly the school felt enormous. I stood there, waiting to hear something, but there was nothing. To pass the time, I had an old computer and a wooden cabinet with glass doors and cloth curtains. I opened it and found a binder covered with blue embossed vinyl, where someone named Raúl Dolores García, who was apparently the school principal for more than twenty years, kept his notes. "El Caín: officially founded on March 11, 1915. Located in the Valley or Lowlands of the stepped Mesetas; rocky terrain, dry climate, with temperatures from a maximum of 35 degrees to a minimum of -14 degrees. There is often snow in winter. One of the worst years was 1948, when the snow reached two meters." Later I found out that these notes are the only recorded history of this town.

• • •

"At home, of course!"

At night, the girls shout out to me from their beds when I ask them, from my bed, if they prefer to be here in town or at home. Not even the electricity and the heat here change their minds. Not even that sometimes they get food here that's not meat. Not even that some parents come to visit them once a week or every two weeks. Not even that afterwards they can go to Maquinchao for high school and then become teachers and who knows what else. No way. They wouldn't trade their homes for anything. The why seems so obvious, it never even comes up. There are ten of them, and they are between six and twelve years old. At night they wait for me, awake, no matter what time I arrive. They peek out from their bunks, and we talk—I, under the scrutiny of pairs of eyes reproduced ad infinitum—for as long as they let us: at any moment, a teacher, who seems like an ogre out of the Brothers Grimm, comes in and turns off the light and orders silence. The teacher makes his nocturnal rounds and checks to see that everything is in order. His presence, like all forms of vigilance, causes more alarm than reassurance.

During the day, all day, I do circuits around the outskirts of town, never stopping. The only thing that could keep me in El Caín itself is the possibility of reading, but I can't find any place to do it. The bunk I was assigned is a bottom bunk, which makes me feel like the ham in a sandwich, so I avoid it until night gives me no other option, and then there are my conversations with the girls. Nor is there any public place where I can settle in with my books; more accurately, there is a bar, but it has nothing remotely like a corner where somebody can sit and read.

Circuit 1: I leave town along the road that reaches Maqui-nchao many kilometers farther on. I leave to take a walk, I say, though the fact is I flee, horrified, from a long and noisy after-dinner conversation. The last thing I managed to hear was a mixture that included: the buzz of two spinning tops shot into a red plastic bucket to battle it out like two fighting roosters + the TV blasting in the background + a zamba about El Caín being performed live: "On the Hill of the Cross / On a peace-ful afternoon / I tarried there to think / On top a rocky cliff / By the side of the road / At the foot of the mountain / You will find the pond / Witness to the fight / Look away into the dis-tance / Toward the light of radiant hope / At the small town standing tall / Struggling for a new tomorrow." How much more peaceful life is in a big city, I conclude. I keep walking and, without meaning to, I begin to verify the words of the zamba, still pulsating inside my head: the hill is there, the cliffs are there, the town is here, and also the pond. The only thing missing is the zamba's epic tone, for when it mentions battle, it refers to the deaths of two of the town's residents, Abraham and Mustafa, at the hands of two bandits, Patiño and Tronco-so, who traveled around this region in the 1920s. The first two, they say, were in the bar one afternoon and, encouraged by the gin and challenged by their fellow customers, they decided to capture Patiño and Troncoso. They soon found them but were also soon frightened away. As they fled, Mustafa and Abraham failed to find the cliffs in time and decided to plunge into the pond. The minute they lifted their heads out of the water to take a breath, the other two killed them without wasting more than one bullet on each. Later, when someone in town tells me that at the time, Troncoso told his grandfather that he and

Patiño "had killed two ducks in the pond," I cannot stop picturing the scene accompanied by the music and the logic of the cartoons I used to watch as a child, cartoons in which blunders are punished with a cruelty that for some reason seemed to be both fair and hilarious.

Circuit II: I drive out of town with Atilio Namuncurá, a relative of Ceferino—the grandson of a great Mapuche warrior who went to Rome to become a priest and is one of Patagonia's most popular saints—who is capable of seeing, even when going more than 140 kilometers per hour, all sorts of nuance where I see only the compact mass of the meseta of Somuncurá. Atilio was born in Chubut, but he considers himself to be Rionegrino, he says. He lives and works in Viedma, though he spends a good deal of time on the road, checking on how things are going in the hamlets and most remote corners of the province. Office hours are apparently the price he pays for these trips. Officially he is a member of the board of the development association, but secretly, I learn, his vocation is as a conversationalist: he knows every single person who lives on this meseta in places where anybody else, at first glance, would say nobody lives, and he is capable of establishing dialogues with them that would be impossible for the rest of us. He knows which subjects to bring up and which to avoid, he can pinpoint the precise moment to tell a joke or to remain quiet for a stretch, and he knows how to find out about their lives without asking a single question. However, he often fails, he tells me. The previous year he came with a professor from the University of Bologna, and the man who lives in the house at our first stop today didn't say a word—he remained totally silent for the hour or more they were there. And we're talking about people who spend months without talking to anybody, people who you might think would be desperate to exchange a few words with anybody. But nothing, not a single word. He didn't even open his mouth to thank him for the bags of wheat, oil, and the rest of the provisions the government distributes once a year to small agriculturalists. He didn't even mention the part about the other being a professor because what possible interest could someone who lives here have in the name of a university or a newspaper or anything else. Nothing, not even a chance. On that day, the man—Lorenzo is his name—sat on a stump he has outside next to the door to his shack—I'll see when we get there—and looked at them as if they were a couple of puppets someone had placed there in front of him to entertain him for a while, a performance to which he had nothing to add. Other times, he simply doesn't show up. One year, Atilio was very worried because he knocked on the door of his shack, of that hovel he lives in, and Lorenzo didn't answer. On the windows, too, and also nothing. He pressed his face against a window in the back and didn't see anybody inside. It was cold: that year they'd gotten a little behind in the distribution of provisions, and winter was approaching. He started looking for him in the surrounding area. Lorenzo lives alone and if one day he goes belly up out there, who knows who'll find him or when. His six goats, the only thing he has, weren't there, either. Maybe, Atilio thought, he died somewhere out there and his goats scattered, having forgotten how to return to the shack. He looked for him everywhere: first on foot, then in his truck, and nothing. Night was approaching, and he decided to leave the bags of flour and other things next to the door, just in case he showed up. He took off, heavy-hearted, thinking that the last time he saw him he should have been more insistent that he go see the doctor in Viedma—he was emaciated, all skin and bones—but it was like telling someone to go to Alaska to see a good dentist. He drove about three kilometers, and there he was, sitting on a rock, surrounded by his six goats, throwing pebbles at other rocks below, down toward the house. It was obvious that from there he could see what was going on at his place, that he'd seen him running around futilely, knocking on doors and windows. As Atilio approached, Lorenzo raised his hand and gave him a half smile, as if to say that there was no need for him to stop.

Circuit III: I leave town on foot and head north, toward where they say there's a gigantic rock that looks like the profile of a woman lying on her back. There's no marked trail, so I feel my way along. The sky is clear and the meseta—interrupted every so often by rock formations that look like smoke from a dense burn—looks like the desert of Wadi Rum that so captivated T. E. Lawrence. A while later, I cross paths with two men on horseback. Nobody greets anybody. The silence is eerie. There's something liberating and at the same time terrifying about walking aimlessly. I pass by a ruin, where the only things standing are two mud walls that form something like a right angle with uncertain boundaries. I lie down to rest—also supine like the sculpted woman who must be around here somewhere—on a flat rock that is at least three times as big as me. That's when the southern lapwings show up. The simple and ubiquitous lapwing, which no geographic formation seems capable of keeping away. They circle, sweep overhead. A while later I continue walking, thinking that there's a pond a little farther on. I decide to make that my goal, the specific destination toward which I am walking, though I continue, and the pond gets farther and farther away. When, at what point during a walk, will that moment arrive that is deemed desirable, when one enters a different state? After the first day, the first week? What mechanism will make the pulse of walking intertwine with the pulse of writing? How did it happen to Monod, Sebald, Thoreau, Lawrence, Patrick Leigh Fermor? Furrows begin to appear in the ground; I assume they are the tracks left by the snowmelt as the water flows toward the pond. Now they're dry so I make them my path. Some, presumably those that carry more water, have eroded so much that they give me the sensation, as I move forward, of sinking between two walls of dry earth that are continually getting higher. I change paths. A herd of horses apparently without an owner gallops toward me. The lapwings return, this time with a frankly rejectionist attitude. When they choose a flight path that points directly at my head, I look around to see if I can find a branch to defend myself. They shout, I shout. The pond remains far away. I pass by many *chupasangres*, bloodsuckers, cactuses that are classified as edible by scientists and in the memory of the indigenous communities, but never in the idiosyncrasy of the contemporary. As the sun sets, I think I've arrived, but a collection of waterlogged grasses dissuades me from reaching the pond itself. I return very late to my bunk bed, but even so, the girls are waiting for me. Máistra, Máistra! Teacher, they always call me, because for them, people who write books are all dead. They want me to tell them all about my day. I invent almost everything, except when they ask me if at some point during my walk I was afraid. I say, yes, yes, I was infinitely terrified of the lapwings. And all of them, in unison, laugh at me. They laugh so hard and so uncontrollably that every once in a while they have to take a deep breath so they can keep on laughing, and I fall asleep to their laughter before they can ask me the next question.

Circuit IV: Again, I drive out of town with Atilio Nauncurá. We take a dirt road, pass through a gate, and park the truck no more than two meters from where a man is working. To the left is the house and toward the right, at the bottom of a bluff—if you can talk about bluffs on a meseta or plateau— there is a large crystal-clear pond. It's definitely a privileged spot, with trees that indicate that someone has been tending it for a long time. We stay in the truck: Atilio wants to prove that his prediction will come true, that the man will pay no attention to us at all, that we could spend the entire afternoon there, and he would keep making his mud bricks without even lifting his eyes to look at us. Those bricks he's making are the most common in this area and are made of a mixture of the soil of the meseta + red clay + water + horse manure, which is used instead of sawdust. Once the ingredients are ready, they are spread over a flat surface, and a horse is made to walk in circles over it until the mixture is thoroughly uniform. At the moment, the man has that mixture in a bucket and pours it over another surface where, Atilio tells me, the bricks will be cut out and left to dry. After pouring out each bucket, the man smoothes the layers with the patience and dedication of a pastry chef. Indeed, at no moment does he turn to look in our direction. But it doesn't appear to be that kind of feigned indifference that ends up costing so much more effort than any kind of greeting; he looks genuinely wrapped up in his world. I figure that because of how much time they spend without anybody else around, these people prove the nonessential nature of the many hours of conversation we hold. A while later—one hour, two hours—we give up and interrupt him. We even manage to get an invitation to enter the house. Atilio puts some logs in the wood-burning stove to liven up the fire. The man says that his name is Gregorio and that he is a *tantero*. Atilio translates: he is not an employee but rather works for a percentage, like a pieceworker. At each pause, when anyone would expect silence, Gregorio whistles. The three of us stand there next to the stove, and he, with his legs stretched out in front of him and his hands in his pockets, whistles and looks up at the ceiling. Atilio says that here, in this hamlet, there's usually a man named Humberto. Gregorio says that he himself hasn't been here long; before he used to work near Río Chico, north of Chubut. (Whistles.) That he never much liked staying in one place, getting attached; he goes somewhere, does his thing, then keeps going down a different road. (Whistles.) That since he's been in this area, he never goes to town, only when he needs a vice. Translation: not just cigarettes and alcohol but also maté, sugar, consumer goods he can't get out in the country. Now the mixture is finished, now he's making the blocks. Translation: bricks. (Whistles.) The problem with the blocks is that you're making them, making sure they're all straight and uniform, and then suddenly it rains, and you've got to start from scratch. Translation: it never rains here, but for the fields, for the sheep, for the grass that never grows, rain is what everybody longs for, and that's why they're always thinking about rain, though sometimes they forget, like in this case, that desire can take the form of misfortune.

Circuit V: I leave town and start walking south, toward where they told me Antonina's house is. I walk about five kilometers along a good path, and there, where the land rises a little, is her house. That's what she told me the previous day, when I made her acquaintance in town. She stopped in her tracks in the middle of the street and shouted at me: what was I doing here. She was carrying some bags: she goes to town to barter her mutton for things she needs in the market. Or for whatever. She barters with the first bidder, the very first one. She was wearing *bombachas de campo*, wide gaucho pants that were at least three times too big for her, and the kind of sheep-fur-lined hat that Antarctic explorers wear. What hat will she wear in winter if this is the hat she wears in November? The same one, my dear, the same one. A hat is a hat. But when I arrive at her house, she's not wearing it, which produces in me the same flurry of strangeness I feel when people who wear glasses take them off to clean the lenses. Come in, my dear, come in. Antonina's house is adobe and has a dirt floor. On a table covered with a faded oilcloth is what will be her topic of the day: a newborn turkey chick the dogs want to eat. The chick is inside a cardboard box, and Antonina has cut an opening in the top to let the air in. The problem is that it can escape through that same opening, she tells me, and she's put that dishcloth over it to prevent the chick from ending up in the maws of one of those starving dogs. While I was in the kitchen the chick must have escaped approximately twenty times from its cardboard cage, the dishcloth fluttering on its head like a superhero's cape. That's life, my dear, that's life. You've got to know how to find shelter, defend yourself. That's why she chased those scoundrels away, knife in hand, the ones who wanted to take her house away from her. With precisely that knife she's now showing me. Antonina lives within the town's public land trust, where a restricted number of animals are allowed without having to pay the fee that is obligatory outside those boundaries. They told her she was disgusting, and that they were going to take her to court to deal with the problem. Ha! Nobody takes her anywhere. She went all by herself. She went in front of the judge, and she turned his brain into mush with everything she told him and said to him. She didn't hold anything back. She even admitted to the part about the knife. How else is a single woman going to defend herself when they want to take away the only things she has and that she's worked so hard to get? Huh, Mr. Judge? The system Antonina has invented to keep the maté water always hot requires a series of steps and several different containers, like an alchemist, and the process doesn't allow her to sit down for even a second throughout our entire conversation. But this doesn't prevent her from remaining focused on what she's saying. The only possible interruption would be the chick, but since I was assigned the task of returning it to its box every time it gets out, it's my problem, so it doesn't distract her, either. And yes, she's thrown men out more or less the same way she threw out those invaders. All useless. Why would she want a man? So some good-for-nothing can give her a hard time because she didn't cook for him? So he can take her to bed every once in a while, then turns out to be soused? So he can help her with the sheep? No, dear, no thanks. As for the bed, she solves that by choosing for herself the moment and the subject, no drunkards and no snoring strangers. And as for the sheep, better not even mention it. Few could do the work as well as she does it. This season things aren't going so well: one lamb ran off and the dogs killed several others. Starving dogs. But, it's obvious, these aren't things a man can make right. No way. She sees the women there in town who have husbands, they all have slouching shoulders and mumble under their breath while the men do whatever they want. No, dear, no way. She doesn't know how men might be in the city, but around here they think we exist to serve them. Ha! The only man she's ever served is her son, who is a wonderful person and is now a policeman in Maquinchao. He comes and visits her whenever he can; he's a good son. Antonina asks me if maybe I can hold the chick for a bit, maybe that way it'll stop jumping around. I hold it with both hands formed into the shape of a bowl and I can feel its heart beating in its fragile body made of half-formed little bones. The chick keeps squealing, and I think how easy it would be to simply clench my fists and make it stop.

Circuit VI: I drive out of town in the ambulance; this time, miraculously, it manages to actually drive. Other times it doesn't have gas, or something is broken and there's no spare part, or the roads are snowy and then they don't make the rounds. The health officer of El Caín thereby enumerates the problems; she's new and doesn't have to contend only with these complications but also with the image of her predecessor, someone named Rosa, who apparently was capable of getting on an old bicycle or riding a guanaco in order to get to wherever she had to go. On this trip there's a doctor, who, I learn, is also a kind of miracle, because in El Caín there are no doctors, just a nurse, and because all the doctors who work in Maquinchao don't want to come out here. This doctor is pretty new in Maquinchao and is very interested in knowing what's going on in the hamlets and remote shacks scattered around the meseta. He's obviously shy and has a preference for out-of-the-way places, two characteristics that often go together, like a toy in a combo meal you didn't ask for but they give you anyway. In the ambulance, as they review the list of people they are going to visit, I finally understand that *parajes*, hamlets, are places that might be considered the vestibules to the towns, where there might even be a school and up to a hundred or so inhabitants, and that *puestos* are isolated houses, or shacks or shanties, where only one family or a single person lives. Sometimes those *puestos* are nearby, like here in the region of Vaca Leufquen, where about seven are located around the pond of the same name. In this first one live Martín Roque and his family. Actually, part of his family, because two of his sons are attending school in Maquinchao, and his wife is there to be with them. They visit very rarely. Martín stayed here with his mother and three other children. One of these three went to school, but when he finished primary school, he came back to the country. The other, who is holding in his arms an orphaned lamb, is a bit disturbed, the father says. Something's wrong with him. They welcome us into the kitchen. They are very hospitable and answer without qualms the questions the health officer asks: if they've had their vaccinations, if there is a woman of reproductive age in the house, if they use contraceptives, if they are sure the dogs don't have tapeworm, if they've seen any kissing bugs in the house. Then the health officer does her job of leaving them vitamins, several basic medicines, milk, and a series of instructions. Nobody writes down the instructions anywhere, so I assume they will forget them as I forget them as soon as we move on to another subject. The vitamins and the medicines, I also assume, will remain untouched in some corner. Noises that sound like gurgling drift into the kitchen. They are from the Cripple, Martín says, who's in the back room. The grandmother goes to her and we follow. The girl is eighteen years old and cannot walk or stand up or speak. She spends her life lying in this room with adobe walls on one of which is a poster of Evita from the fifties. The health officer tries to convince them to take her outside into the fresh air on these nice days, allow her to participate in their daily activities. The grandmother grabs her hand, the girl stops gurgling and looks at her as if the totality of her world were concentrated in that contact. It's clear they will die together. Through the window can be seen the vegetable garden, everything in neat rows and surrounded by a well-maintained fence. It's Grandma who carries her, says one of the boys. The grandmother is eighty-five years old, her skinniness contrasting visibly with the energy she radiates, and she's wearing a pair of earrings with green stones, which she must wear all the time because our visit was unannounced.

Circuit VII: I leave town with Melivilo, the development commissioner from El Caín. We head for Barril Niyeu, the hamlet where he was born and where the monthly meeting of hamlets over which he always presides will be held. We arrive at the school, which is the venue for the meeting and the hub of communal life. The issues to be discussed, Melivilo says in front of a group of fifteen men and women who hail from the surrounding areas, are: 1) health, 2) the school cafeteria, 3) the children's excursion to Las Grutas, 4) miscellaneous news, 5) schedule change for the monthly meeting. Among the fifteen attendees only one offers opinions, engages in the discussion, makes suggestions. The rest are sprawled out in their chairs with blank looks on their faces, as if all of this had absolutely nothing to do with them. I also sprawl out in the desk they've given me. In the seat next to me I manage to read, in the report the husband of the director is writing: need to pave Route 23 to prevent increased isolation of hamlets . . . the southern sector of Río Negro has been losing population, according to the last report created by the Development Agency for the Southern Region . . . review conditions of small agriculturalists relative to AFIP, Argentina's IRS . . . new developments regarding deductions for exports . . . rounds made by health officers to the hamlets have decreased in the last few months . . . problems with the ambulance, old and has no spare parts . . . need to turn directly to Department of Public Health to expose shortfalls . . . problem of distance vis-à-vis the authorities who might hear these complaints . . . permission for the children to go on excursion to Las Grutas in December . . . policemen in El Caín responsible for taking them from Barril Niyeu to Maquinchao, where they can catch the bus. I paid particular attention to this point, about the children's excursion, because I was certain that I would hear the women speak up about it. The director, a policeman, and Melivilo tried to set the day and time for departure, they talked about what the kids were going to do, about how important it was for them to see the ocean, to take a train for the first time in their lives, but the women did not contribute a single word. In these places it's not unusual to find children who suffer from labor and sexual abuse, a child psychologist who is taking a trip around the region whispers to me, and she assures me that she knows about more than one case of a man trading his daughter for a herd of goats. And here I thought that this was something that happened only in the desert in the Middle East, which this meseta reminds me of. At this meeting is Rosa, the assistant health officer they told me about a few days ago; she stands on her chair and holds forth, saying that what happened the other day just can't keep happening, that a boy came to them from a hamlet having convulsions and they had to go to El Caín to call Maquinchao by radio to figure out how to get him to the hospital, because as everybody knows it's the only hospital around, and all the radios responded—all of them, she says, as she pauses to sweep her eyes over those who are sitting around her, turning her head in a circle as if it were the scope of a submarine peering out over the water—absolutely all of them responded except the one in Maquinchao, and then the Choele Choel Civil Defense Force had to call the police in Los Menucos so they could get closer to Maquinchao with a truck, and so forth. And then, well, she's not sure, but she wouldn't be surprised if it was just one more instance of the folks in Maquinchao turning off their radios because the buzzing disturbed them while they were watching the game. I go out to get some fresh air. Strolling around outside, it doesn't take long before I find what they call here "the indigenous cemetery." It consists of a collection of graves surrounded by a low mud wall, about waist-high. All the grass is overgrown as if there were no descendents or public entity to take care of it. Some of the graves—of those who died in the twenties or thirties—are marked with an iron cross of an austere, subtle design. I wonder what might have become of the person who made them, how he acquired that aesthetic sensibility, and if he had taken precautions to make sure that his grave would also sport one of those crosses, even if his own death would occur decades later. As usually happens with abandoned or low-budget cemeteries, the ground is uneven, full of those little mounds that make it seem like someone is moving around inside the graves. That's why, I suppose, people pay fortunes to be buried in private cemeteries, so the perfectly flat grounds can create the fantasy that their dead are resting in peace. A hare bursts out of the overgrown grass but doesn't startle me.

The grocery store, the infirmary, the court, the police station, the telephone booth, the office of the commissioner, and the bar are the places you can go in El Caín. I go to the bar. It's almost eight o'clock, the hour when the women cook and the men get together to play cards, a game called *truco*. The men, today, are not just any group; one could say that around this table are the representatives of the political class and the dynamic forces if the dimensions of the town hadn't converted them all into pompous but empty titles. I sit down in a chair next to the table where they are all playing standing up. A while later, I look toward the door and see the glass crowded with the faces of children: thick glass in constant motion, like a hive. Somebody tells me that they are staring because women don't come into the bar. They, the players, weren't shocked when I entered because by now I've already interviewed all of them, they already know me. The same isn't true for the owner of the bar, whose extreme deafness turns him into a nearly impenetrable fortress. He understands all of them, the school director explains to me, through signing and the strength of habit. They lift a hand and a gin appears, they move their head and the peanuts show up. I make the mistake of asking for a coke with fernet—a synthesis would have increased my chances of obtaining the object of my desire, but I order a composite drink of which the barman hears only the part about the coke. The man has no teeth and I suspect that under his beret he doesn't have any hair, either. He watches the others play with almost childlike attention, and he misses the most interesting part of *truco*: what is being said.

She was a hot woman and she was sipping Knorr soup / A *truco*, already? / Okay, hit me / They take him to the potty like he's a baby / Come on, play / A dead man can't drown / And if you don't drown, you lose / Hit me / You still kicking? / I don't like this game 'cause I don't tell lies / *Flor, che* / Good play / Oh no! / Another *flor* / She had a boy / I'll betcha a hundred sheep / Hey, are we playing *truco* or what? / *De punto y hacha dijo la vizcacha* / Come on, come on, do I hear any bids? / Why are they dating if he can't score? / *Envido* / Did you call?

• • •

It's impossible: it's definitely impossible for me to read in El Caín. I can't stop walking from place to place, roaming around.

If I stay still, without a book, I'm afraid of being captured by the upper bunk bed or by the teacher making his rounds or by the freewheeling announcer on a television program or by a housewife who wants to tell me her life story. That's why I get up early and take off. Wherever. Years ago I left here, the South, to a large extent because of the lack of books, something I also already said. And then, with time, I have been able to survive each and every one of my visits thanks to the books I bring with me to read—or those I find, because it turns out not to be true that there weren't any books, but that's another story. Books function for me like a voucher given upon entry: a password that means I can leave at any moment. This town, where I can't read, is bringing to the surface that old anxiety, that fear of being trapped. Or perhaps, I tell myself, it has nothing to do with some old affliction but rather a more recent affliction: by coming to Caín I have fallen victim to the toponymy, and am now condemned to wander for life. "Wandering and perpetually afraid." Like Vigeland's Cain: surrounded by people and even a dog, from whom, however, he is completely disconnected, unaware of his role in caring for them, terrified, nothing but skin and bones, his crazed eyes that never blink because in them he has placed all his hope of discovering where the fatal blow will come from. From the pages of the notebook covered in blue embossed vinyl that contain a record of the history of the town, the ornate calligraphy of the school principal-historian attempts to dissuade me: "El Caín," it says, is a distortion of "iëlkaiên," the name the northern Tehuelche gave to a particular stone used for grinding. And he adds: "Hence we must dismiss explanations based on derivations from Araucano and Spanish, these last, of Biblical origin." Just when these as-

sertions are on the verge of reassuring me, I think about Melivilo, a name that reminds me of the other aspect of whales:
not the docile animal that sustains a large portion of the tour-
ism industry in Patagonia, but rather the other, Melville's, that
monster who demands to be constantly pursued.

EIGHT

It turns you into a loner, that's the problem with this job. Compared to how he was when he started, he could even be called a hermit. Yes, that's probably what he is now. To think that he comes from a huge family with seven siblings, not counting all the cousins, and all the friends to boot. In his house, there was always a lot of noise, people talking, music. His father loved music, especially classical. Schubert, Wagner, he doesn't really remember what others. To tell the truth, he never really took to it. Since they—he and his siblings—were big on inviting people over, his father would sometimes have enough already and listen with his headphones. There he'd be, stretched out in an armchair, while everything passed over him, around him. And he with his serene smile, impervious, protected by his headphones that looked like those pom-pom earmuffs female skiers from the States wear, with bright colors and little flair skirts. He never really understood how the simple fact of listening to music could transform a person in that way. But there are so many things about other people we don't understand, especially about our parents. How often he thought about it, about him, that is, about his father, while he was wandering around out there in the fields, on so many nights. Everything

he never understood and, at the same time, that never occurred to him to ask. That's the thing about this job, Federico
says, doubling back: you've got to spend eight, even ten hours
straight going from one oil well to another, alone—often alone,
most of the time alone—and there are times when everything
is going perfectly, you're doing exactly what you're supposed
to be doing, checking to make sure that everything is in order, that there are no spills, that the bolts are all tightened, but
there are other times when your mind wanders, it refuses to see
that a bolt is a bolt and instead starts to ask these kinds of questions. Why was it that his father could only achieve that kind
of serenity with music and why was it that he was an alcoholic.
To put it simply, he tells me, there are days when the questions
enter his head and since there's nobody to answer them out
there, as he's going from well to well, he ends up answering
them himself, or something like that. And so when later he
runs across somebody, it doesn't make sense to ask them again.
That's what he meant about becoming a loner: it's a job that
forces you to permanently make do on your own, and then,
when others show up, you no longer have anything to say to
them or ask them or tell them, and you gradually start realizing
that there's less and less you need from them.

At first, when he started doing this, they usually went out into
the fields in a group. And he even enjoyed that. He'd just left
home, as he already told me, and he was used to doing everything in a pack. To think, it was his first job ever, and now
to think that he's been at it for around ten years. Sometimes,
when he remembers how it happened that he came there,
he wonders if it's not some kind of revenge against his family

that makes him keep doing it; other times he honestly thinks that there's no job that could possibly make him happier than spending all day, or all night, out in the oil fields. By now at home they've gotten used to it, but at first it caused an uproar. The only one who never turned a hair was his father, but anyway he's dead now. He still remembers the day he told him. In fact, it's the only thing he remembers clearly: the reaction of the rest of his family is like a uniform cackling that time has left behind, it never comes back to him, not even in his most far-flung nightmares. But the memory of his father has remained intact. It must be because of his deep-seated fear of him, even though his father never raised his voice and never said anything insulting to him. He was afraid of disappointing him, not afraid of him. That's what it's really about. It was a summer day, he remembers, and the heat from outside combined with the heat from the kitchen, where they were talking. It was seven in the evening, something like that, the time of day when his father always started cooking. For everybody, every night. He came from his office, took off his jacket and tie, put on an apron that every once in a while he allowed somebody to wash, and started cooking for everybody. And he poured himself a whiskey. That day Federico offered to pour him one, he remembers. His father gave him a strange look: even though he knew that Federico was the only one who didn't get nervous when he walked through the house with his glass, with that exaggerated pretense of being in control that alcohol sometimes produces, he also knew that it had never occurred to him to pour him a shot. But he continued anyway, as if it were nothing, cutting the vegetables, the pancetta, the chorizo. He said thanks and that was all. That day he was making a stew he'd learned from his mother; he insisted that it was typical of the region in Germany where his family was from. Nobody at home believed him, but he insisted that that night they would eat the stew from the forest of Thüringer. He said that his family came from the forest, and that's why, after graduating, he settled there, in Esquel, but there are several family theories about this that don't always jive. It's true that he'd chosen to settle in Esquel, but not that he came from the forest, because even his grandfather had been born here, in Argentina, in Catamarca. So there was the heat in the kitchen, and because of some auspicious coincidences, none of his siblings or cousins or friends were there that day. Not in the kitchen, at least, though Federico remembers their voices as background noise. His three youngest siblings, the only ones who still lived at home; his two brothers were at the university in Buenos Aires, and his sister was already married to the richest man in town. Federico said it as a fait accompli: a plan, something already arranged. He told him that the following week he was going to Santa Cruz Province to work in the oil fields. He said that two days before he'd received word that he'd gotten the job. His father didn't alter a single one of his movements. Federico remembers that to make the stew he would chop the vegetables very small, and that on that specific day he thought it was strange that neither the alcohol nor his announcement had made his father's hands shake. His father finished chopping and put it all into the pot—which he didn't usually do—and he took that moment, when his back was turned, to say: "Good plan. Too bad there are no trees there, in northern Santa Cruz." That's the only thing he said. And Federico left the following Monday, as he said he would, except that he had no contract, no nothing.

And then, over the years, with each visit home, his father never said another word about it. He asked him the usual questions, largely the same ones he asked his other sons who came to visit from Buenos Aires and who, today, are doctors and lawyers. Federico sincerely believes that was all he had to say about it.

At first, as he was saying, they would go out to the oil fields in groups. It was a different era: back then, he needed that. Now, it's different. If he sees that a well, for example, isn't flowing as it should, he goes and makes the adjustments that he has to make on the rods, the pump, whatever, and that's that, problem solved. Before, when this was YPF, before his time, pumpers like him would go around, and the only thing they did was carry their spreadsheet and then send the information to the supervisor, who in turn would send it to the area manager. Now, it's different. The companies, mostly North American, train one person to be able to deal with everything that might happen, both above and below the well. Someone who is capable of making sure that the ball bearings on the crankshafts aren't making any noise, that the strobe lights are working, but also capable of working in that underground world: there, under that pump, he points, there might be a well that's up to 2,500 meters deep. Twenty-five hundred. The oil and gas, like pampered passengers, are carried to the surface from more than twenty blocks straight down. You've got to deal with the rods, the *casing*, the *tubing*. He uses the English words but doesn't even try to pronounce them correctly. It's a way of working that's spreading. And, to tell the truth, he thinks it's a good thing. Less bureaucracy, fewer out-of-order telephones. But, obviously, then there's that other thing that he was talking about at the beginning, that issue about dealing with everything alone. It has its pros and its cons.

The night shift was always his favorite. Driving around out in the country in a Ford F100 with the wind whistling through the windows; the old men with their hats and gloves, tired, waiting for the moment when they stop at the *carpa*. Here in Santa Cruz, they call the wood shacks built by YPF *carpas*, tents, and an "old man" was anybody over twenty. They say old man instead of "guy" or "bloke" as a colloquial way of referring to someone. There was always an old man there who was cooking something to eat, but seriously cooking. None of this heating up some leftover soup. Everybody's favorite was Gordo Martínez, who had a new recipe every week. Gordo's wife died giving birth to their second child, and he was raising his kids like gods. And to do that you have to know how to cook, he always said. And he treated all of them a little like his own kids, as well. When Federico met him, Gordo wasn't going out to the fields anymore; he had only two years left till retirement. Sometimes they'd be late because there'd been a problem at one of the wells—a bolt that needed adjusting, a clogged pipeline, one of those things you can't put off till later—but whenever they'd arrive, Gordo would be there, steadfast, with the food ready and never an expression of worry or irritation on his face. For Federico, this was priceless: to know that in that place, where it seems like the only thing you're going to find is an oil pump, another puddle of spilled oil, another dry clump of grass, there is actually someone there waiting for you with food ready. And with something strong to drink, to restore your energy, your faith. It was prohibited, of course, but they always managed to camouflage something in the truck, and to keep a kind of permanent stock in some corner of the *carpa*. Some in the group had found a perfect hiding place for the bottles between two planks they'd used to build walls to better keep out the wind. They'd found a corner where there was one plank that could be removed and then put back without anybody noticing. At least Gordo pretended not to notice: he almost never said anything about what they were drinking and, if he did, he'd refer to "those things they were carrying." Federico thinks that since he's been living in Santa Cruz he's never had something more like a home than that *carpa* in the middle of the fields. To be out there in the open country with the certainty that somewhere someone was waiting for him, that's a home. And that's considering that often there were delays of hours rather than minutes—two, three, five hours. At first he thought that Martínez's ability to wait for so long was something unique to him, but after all these years he's realized that this work instills in you a very particular notion of time. To go into the fields is to go into another dimension. After a while, you're overtaken by a kind of daze, a stupor, not because of anything in particular. A kind of bliss, even if I might think he's exaggerating. Which doesn't prevent me from acknowledging that we've been roaming around the meseta for only two hours, and I can already intuit how the things that are going through my mind are somehow remote. I remember that this also happens to me sometimes when I ride the #60 bus in Buenos Aires, but here I perceive a difference. As if I were facing the quality of remoteness in its pure state, applied to nothing or nobody in particular. It must have something to do with going from one place to another, always looking at pumps that are rising and falling. The mind gets stripped of whatever it was carrying around inside it, and little by little it starts paying attention only to that: the combination of circular and pendular movements. It provokes a kind of hypnosis.

Other times, they'd amuse themselves by looking through the fields for people fucking. They'd shine the headlights of the F100 and wouldn't leave them alone until they showed their faces. Now he can't believe he thought that was fun. It's another thing he owes to this job: the fact that he cares less and less about other people's lives. What happened once at the house of one of the ranchers around here must also have had an effect, the owners of one of the fields where they pump oil. Most of them don't live here, in these houses. They charge the companies a good easement for the land, and they live in Río Gallegos, or in Comodoro, or even in Buenos Aires. They leave the caretakers here in these country houses, and they go elsewhere. Especially in recent years. It's understandable: they spent years trying to survive off sheep shearing and, suddenly, come the nineties, conditions began to greatly improve because of how much they received from the oil companies to dig on their land. But those people, that family Federico is talking about, they never left their country house. At most, sometimes, they go to Comodoro and spend a few days, never even a full week. They like being here. They came years ago from Spain, made money in trade in the Comodoro region, then bought a thousand hectares in Santa Cruz. The one who did leave as soon as she could was their only daughter. First she went to Buenos Aires and then to Europe, to France. When she left to study at the university, her parents sold their businesses and came to live almost full time in the country, so they'd been there for more than ten years when all that happened. Their daughter came for the holidays. It's not at all usual for the oil workers to come into contact with the owners of the leased fields, but Federico's case is different in this way, too. During that period, when he still needed to be around people, he would stop by at some of the houses. At this one in particular: the owners were always there, and they kind of adopted him. When Federico was out there alone, he'd go visit them and it didn't matter what time of day he arrived, they were always happy to welcome him, almost like the son they'd never had. He even spent the night there, at the house, once in a while. They told him all about Spain, about how they'd gotten their start in Comodoro, in the fifties, and he told them about his fellow oil workers, about his family, about his brothers. It was a little like going back to Esquel, though quieter, of course. And in some ways warmer, which was hard to admit. Through that couple, and the nights he'd sit up talking with them, he realized that cracks were starting to show in the great big united family that he'd always been so sure of having. One day, he remembers, he was driving back at night after having been at their house, and without meaning to he realized that his mother had always been too worried about measuring how many more centimeters the arrival of each new child made her breasts sag, and that his father, hiding behind his headphones or his glass of whiskey or his intricate recipes, was always absent. That night, he felt that for the first time someone had listened to him. He doesn't mean by this, Federico explains, that he blames his parents for anything; he just wants to express how much affection he had for those people. Until that night when their daughter arrived, whom he'd never met.

Except in photographs, of course: school prom photos, gradua-
tion photos, photos on airplane boarding ramps, beach photos
with palm trees, skiing photos, all kinds of photos. He didn't
know she would be there that night; it had been about a month
since Federico had been in that field, and apparently the girl
had shown up a little unexpectedly, even for her parents. She
was also pretty in person, but she didn't smile as much as in
the photos. Her legs were very shapely and her hands were
long. But that's not why he got close to her, nothing to do with
desire. He's convinced—and this is one of the subjects that he's
mulled over in his head the most throughout the years, while
he's out in the field—he's now convinced that he got close to
her, at first, to give her a lesson, to set her straight. Could even
be to punish her. Out of a desire to punish her. It always sur-
prises him that so many things can happen in so little time.
Though maybe it wasn't so little time, he's not sure. What
bothered him that first night was that her presence brought
tension to the table, and what was usually a spontaneous and
familial conversation suddenly felt like an office meeting. He
could never stand those things, much less in a place that felt to
him like home. She was an intruder.

A few nights later, Federico returned, because they formally invited him to dinner, as they had never done before. The tense
atmosphere was just like the first time, or even worse. As if the
passing of days, instead of making things more relaxed, had
made the air even thicker. He noticed it in the mother's relief
when she opened the door after he knocked. Because that night
he knocked; other nights he'd just clap his hands together a
couple of times and go in. At a certain point he felt like he'd

been hired to liven up the evening, lighten the burden of not knowing what to do, what to say, how to mitigate the presence of the intruder. He had no intention of intervening in any way in what was going on there; in the end, it wasn't his storyline no matter how much he wanted it to be. Until he saw the face she, the daughter, made: it was a second, a split second, but who knows why it irritated him so much. Over the years since then, it's happened, he'd be out in the field, and he'd close his eyes and find himself again in that scene—clear, undimmed, a piece of gunk that got in his eye and never left. They'd already eaten and the two women insisted on going into a kind of sitting room to have coffee, a room he'd never entered. He said that first he went to the bathroom, and when he returned he saw the two of them, mother and daughter, but they didn't see him. The father wasn't there, he must have stayed a while longer in the kitchen to somehow show his opposition to this change of ritual. The mother, at the very moment he was entering the cold sitting room, was placing the tray with the cups of coffee on a small table, and she, the daughter, who was sitting in one of the armchairs, almost didn't wait for her to finish setting it down before she started removing the teaspoons the mother had placed inside the cups. She removed them, dried them with a napkin, and placed them on the saucer, next to the cups. If you paid attention only to her hands, which were long and lovely, it seemed she was doing it as if it were just one more chore, but the problem was in her eyes: she was looking at her mother with infinite scorn for what she'd done with the teaspoons. Then she looked from side to side, as if at an invisible audience, and then she looked at him, who was staring at her in shock. The mother stood still, next to the tray, like a child who'd just been reprimanded, as if convinced that her body was too awkward to move among those armchairs and those teacups. Neither of them said anything. He left as soon as he could, thinking that he wouldn't go back for a long time, not until he was sure that she'd be long gone. But he returned the next day and the one after that and then he thinks there were three more times, until what happened happened, and he never returned. Not when she was there and not when she'd left. He lost those people who treated him like a son. And all for someone like that. Another thing he's asked himself so many times while out there, in one of those trucks he drives now, that has shock absorbers and no wind blowing in through the windows: how could he be attracted to such a small-minded, superficial person like her. She was one of those typical people who, when they leave a town, return with some kind of superiority complex; there are a lot of them here, in the South. He even noticed some of that in his brothers, when they'd return for vacation, but it was much less pronounced. No comparison. That day, the day with the coffee, what he couldn't stand was the contrast. The contrast between what her parents had said, how they'd bragged about her, and what really took place later when they were together. It was too much for him, maybe because in his own way, he'd also abandoned his family and who knows what they'd say about him, and what would happen, really, when he visited them. Anyway, he visited them less and less. It's also one of the consequences of this job. When he first started, it seemed like he had so many things to tell them. New things about the job, the people he was meeting. It was, also, a familiar house to return to. Now, since his father died, each brother lives in his own house, and each time he returns there's a big fuss, figuring out who he's going to stay with, for how many days, who first, who next. The worst part is that after all these years, he's incapable of figuring out if part of this fuss is a desperate desire to own him, to have him all to themselves when he visits, or the opposite, if he's become so much of a black sheep that nobody knows where to hide every time he shows up.

• • •

It happened little by little. During his first visits to his brothers, he'd start to talk about something, and after three sentences, he'd feel scattered, he would even say, exhausted. As if they'd told him to move some bags of cement and recite Our Lord's Prayer, which he didn't even remember, while carrying the bags on his shoulders. That's what it is: a mixture of effort, duty, and forgetfulness. Because to this day he has to admit that he honestly doesn't remember what kind of information gets exchanged around a table where there are fifteen, twenty people who turn out to be, each in his or her own way, members of your family. He doesn't remember. During those visits when he started experiencing that kind of amnesia, it was as if his family was speaking the same language that he'd learned along with them, and he was the only one who'd forgotten it. That's why he would make such an effort. Because he thought it was his fault, his own fragile memory. Somehow, honestly, it seemed like he was the traitor. But it was inevitable: he'd bring up some subject, and even if when he started it seemed like he'd taken the right track, that this anecdote might interest them, suddenly he'd look at all of them sitting there around the table, and he'd notice that some were making an effort to pay attention while others, especially the women, would turn to give instructions to a child or get up to bring or take away plates, desserts, drinks. He honestly couldn't figure out how to stay focused himself or to get others to focus on him. Not even his mother, who'd interrupt him in the middle of his sentences and ask him if he'd finally found a girl out there who was more or less worthy of him, when might he give her a tenth grandchild.

During one of those visits he decided to resign himself to it, stop making an effort. He thought that if he didn't manage to talk, at least he would make sure to listen. But he immediately felt like he was in a daze, like he'd been buried in an avalanche. Like he used to feel when he was a child and his mother would force him to organize his closet: he'd drag his heels, resign himself to it, and five minutes later he'd feel furious and helpless, trying to duck from everything that overwhelmed him as soon as he summoned up the courage to open those doors. They were large and painted white, he remembers. Mention of school, of the office, of the neighbors, the children's shouts, the questions nobody wanted answers to, the repetitions, the instructions, the old aggressions, undimmed, superfluous details that lead to the banal central anecdote, the inquisitions, rivalries, constant self-references, the children's achievements, the children's outbursts, criticism of the maids, dependence on the maids, marital discord, tones of voice, unnecessary irritations, the feeling that, deep down, everybody was talking to themselves. That's why he prefers this: the fields, the wells, the truck, the serenity of talking to himself, knowing he's alone, without having to make up a bunch stories to hide that fact. It's not that people no longer interest him, not at all. It's just that he realized that he has less and less to say. Or maybe he distills it better. He asks for what he needs, he expresses gratitude, he states a fact. Period. The rest gets resolved in his head when he's out in the field. Long conversations, let's say. That's why he can tell these things to me, because I agreed to come out there with him and because, honestly, for him it's like talking to himself, except that this time he's talking out loud. No offense intended. For him this isn't very different from what usually goes on in his head. Sometimes he remembers clearly the fight he had with that woman, the one with the long hands. After what happened, they said everything to each other, and he took the opportunity to tell her what he'd seen that day with the coffee, to tell her in detail exactly how superficial and small-minded she was. She told him that he saw visions and was a lost soul. And later, many years later, he's had to admit that there was something prophetic in that sentence, that still today he sometimes sees visions and feels completely lost.

NINE

Martina says she knows what a child suffers before getting to that point. A pure state of suffering, that's what it is. Because at that age life is something you live, not something you think about, much less question. The same goes for death. In order to kill yourself at that age you have to have experienced a magnitude of suffering that nobody can imagine. A magnitude that makes you obsessed with the idea of putting an end to everything, absolutely everything, and with nothing else. You don't have it in you to think about anything else. Later, when you're older, it's different: you think you know what death is, you've created your own fantasies, and also you have some idea, already formed, about what you'd be exposing yourself to if you kill yourself. But at that age it's different; suicide is like a cause without any effect: ending the suffering isn't associated with ending everything. It's different, very different, people don't understand it and can't imagine it. She does; but more than imagine it, she actually knows it. Before she was twelve, she'd tried to kill herself three times. Martina has had a hard life, a very hard life. They wouldn't dare come to her with their moralizing and speechifying. She'd tell those folks who go around casting aspersions on those kids, treating them almost like lowlifes because they kill themselves, she'd tell them to try for once to feel that despair, which is like a sharp whistling sound that saps you from the inside. Let them feel it way down deep and then talk, if, that is, they still have it in them to go around criticizing others. Martina already wrote two novels so she could get everything she lived through off her chest, and she's going to give me one to take with me. Yes, yes, even though it hasn't been published. She's not a fan of holding things in.

> We piece together our real life in our own way, sometimes it can be a verse, poetry, a poem, or simply what we want it to be . . . I know so much about losing, and nothing about winning. It's just as risky as being a mountain climber. I like to take bold risks, ones that mean a lot, to live dangerously, to fight against the traps life sets.
>
> *excerpt from Martina's unpublished novel*

About ten vials of poison: that's what she took the first of the three times. She was nine years old and worked in the house of a magistrate, in Sarmiento. Martina was born out in the country near Facundo, the daughter of a Tehuelche mother and a German father. German Jew. But she always felt Tehuelche, in spite of all the dirty tricks her mother played on her. Pure Tehuelche, otherwise she would never have survived what happened to her. The magistrate's house is where she landed when her parents separated. Her father took off, and she didn't see him for years, and then her mother left, as well. Though unfortunately she did see her again, later, on many occasions. What's more, she still sees her. But mother *mother*, actually, for her there's only Mother Teresa. The sun pours in through the window of the room where Martina has her bed, her television, a table on which she works on the sculptures she learned how to make by herself, all by herself. The sun shines directly on the oversized plaster arm Mother Teresa raises in a triumphant gesture. The thing is, when both her parents took off, one to the North and the other to the South, she had to go live with strangers. First was that magistrate, then a policeman, then a military man, and so on. They hired her to work for them. That time with the vials of poison, that was the first time.

The magistrate let her go to school only if and when she finished all the household chores. She had to get up before five in the morning, when it was still dark out, so she'd have time to clean everything and catch the bus that came at seven thirty and took the kids to the school that was pretty far away. She remembers being there so many times, rushing around, thinking she'd make it in time, when suddenly she'd see the bus go by, and there she was, still holding the broom. Often she'd miss it by just a little. Maybe she'd have cleaned the bathroom, the kitchen with all those pots and pans stuck with grease from the night before, she'd have made the beds, and she only had to mop the floor in the entryway to make it shine, even though very few visitors ever entered there, but they were visitors nonetheless. But not even then could she make it. There was nothing to do, no point in begging. The magistrate was strict. Everything finished meant everything finished, he told her once, and she immediately understood. She can still clearly remember those situations; more than remember, she can see herself as if she were in one of those instant photos they take nowadays. There she is, drying the glasses, counting only seven left, and the bus driving past the window; or twisting the floor rag to do a final pass and the bus driving past the window. And so forth. After a while, the bus began to lend a different magnitude to her actions. What she was doing automatically, without thinking, as just one more morning chore, suddenly took on a weight of its own. Wringing out the floor rag had stopped being just that and became the reason she was late and therefore the reason she would suffer one more day: an act with such consequence that it deserved to be observed in all its details. The signs, for example, that indicated that it was time to wring it out—that the rinse water came out clear or no more hairs were stuck to it—or the different ways of wringing it out, folding it in two or holding it by both corners like an accordion. It wasn't trivial. On the one hand, it made her sad to miss the bus, miss the chance to be there with the teacher, who was so kind to her, and with the other kids, who made her laugh all the time, and the idea of drinking those glasses of warm milk, fresh from the cow. How could it not make her sad to miss all that. But more than sadness, which always passes with the tiniest bit of joy, what worried her was the terror of going crazy at seeing the bus drive by so many times. The idea that the bus would make every act, every thing, start to crumble into an infinite number of pieces in her mind, without her being able to do anything to stop it. That the world around her would turn into one of those Chinese boxes where one thing contains another, and so on indefinitely.

• • •

The point is that this is what was going on when one day the magistrate asked her to clean out the garage he had behind the house, where he kept the car, tools, all those things that men love to accumulate. And he says to her: Martina, be careful with those vials there, they're poison. Be sure that when you take them out to clean, the dogs don't get them. The dogs. As soon as he got into his car with his family—it was a Sunday, they were going out for a drive, so that day she didn't even need to keep watch for the bus—she grabbed the vials and drank all of them. The last thing she remembers is that she was still drinking, then nothing. Nothing, a total blank. She woke up in a bed in the hospital in Sarmiento. The magistrate was a good man, in his own way. She saw his horrified face when she opened her eyes, as if at least for a moment he was concerned about her. But then he didn't want her in his house anymore, he told her that he didn't like leaving and not knowing what he was going to find when he got back. His wife didn't give her opinion. The kids less so. So she went from one house to another. Forget about school, obviously. Always working, and in between trying to kill herself.

> The fable of the dinner table, where you say, mommy, pass me the bread, or daddy, I want a glass of soda, so simple and sweet. So sweet it makes you think.
> *another excerpt from the same unpublished novel*

So, at sixteen she said yes to the first man who asked her to marry him. Finally, she wouldn't have to work in other people's houses. And at first she thought she was the happiest woman in the world. The man who'd proposed to her was none other than the singer of Frutilla de Cristal, a band that was very much in vogue all through the South. A sight for sore eyes, he was; she was so proud and if she'd had a friend for sure she would have envied her the husband she'd found. He was modern, he wore wide bell-bottom pants. The other girls had boyfriends who spent all day in those coveralls, working the wells, their hands greasy, full of oil, while she had finagled herself a guy who wore colorful pants and had perfectly groomed hands. He smoked, and when he was up on stage, all the girls screamed with excitement. She didn't go much to see him sing—he said a wife should stay at home—but she remembered the one time she did go, at the beginning. At the beginning: that phrase gives her the shivers. For her, getting married meant not cleaning other people's houses anymore; she never imagined any other consequences. Her mother—her own mother—had still not reappeared in her life, she'd already told me she didn't have any girlfriends, and the people she worked for never talked to her. Not even the women in those houses explained the facts of life to her. Nothing. Anyway, those women didn't talk much, not even with their husbands, not with anybody. And anyway, what could they know about life. Martina has the impression that in general people talk more now, maybe because of TV, she doesn't know, but at that time, they didn't. Or maybe it's because now she lives here, in Las Heras, which is a city, so people here are more apt to talk. It's mostly to badmouth others, but at least they're talking. But before, when she lived in the country, really out in the country, out there people didn't even open their mouths. Those women in small towns, they don't talk, either. The thing about the beginning, as she was saying, is that everything fell on her like a ton of bricks, and she wasn't prepared, not at all. It's as if they'd suddenly sent her to, say, Japan, and right after she got there they told her to invite friends over for dinner and make some typical Japanese food and tell them all about life in that little town in Osokama—or whatever it's called, that one from the war. Like that, that's how marriage was at first for Martina. She still remembers the exact moment. It was night, and it was cold. She'd met the man who would be her husband the week before she married him, the man whose name she'd rather not say or even remember, and the thing is, they'd only ever seen each other during the day. So, this was the first night they spent in what would be their little nest. They had a little house—well, a rented room with a bathroom and a kitchen—and that's where they were that first night. It was cold outside, and inside, too. The kind of cold that sinks into your bones. She remembers that they'd eaten something at the local dive, because it was a special day, and she remembers that when they entered the little house, the first thing she felt was a wave that brought back all the other houses where she'd spent her life: the magistrate's, the policeman's, the military man's. That is, other people's houses. Wasn't marriage supposed to liberate her from that? She put down the small bag that contained all her clothes and sat down in a chair, some kind of old armchair that was there in the room. She was about to put away her clothes when suddenly she saw that her husband, the same one who made all the girls scream when he sang, was naked. Just like that. She looked at him from her armchair, in shock. This guy is nuts, she thought. To get undressed right there in front of her, even with them having a bathroom, which they'd paid extra to get. She already was starting not to like him. That night he laughed at her a lot, better said, it was the first night that he laughed at her a lot because that became the constant in her marriage. He laughed nonstop. He laughed at her for being bewildered in that chair, he laughed but he didn't explain anything. That night, when he got tired of laughing, he got angry. And she slept in the armchair, where it continued to be cold.

I'm not innocent at all, nor would I want people to think or believe I am, because I know how to stab my eyes into the eyes of another individual as if they were daggers.

another excerpt

She had four children, all of them with him, the pop star, and not because she was in love—or fond of him, to tell the truth, she wasn't even fond of him—but because she didn't want her kids to go through what she had gone through, having a mother who had children with whoever happened to be around. It wasn't long before she understood that what he wanted that night, the first night of their marriage, was for her to get into bed with him and for everything that has to happen to happen, and after a while she started feeling bad, really, really bad. Her head hurt, she was vomiting, really bad. She went to the clinic in Sarmiento, where they were living, and the doctor said that she was pregnant. He didn't laugh, because he was a doctor, but Martina realized that when he saw that she didn't understand the relationship between what happened in bed with the pop star and this business of having a baby in her belly, he made a face that was more or less like the one her husband had made that first night. Martina didn't tell her husband right away; she was afraid he'd take it badly. He continued with his life as usual. Things didn't change. When they got into bed, she suffered double because now added to the unpleasantness and the pain was this vomiting thing. A thousand times she had to hold her mouth tightly closed so as not to vomit on that pop star's curly locks. What an outrage that would have been, because he had his shampoo brought to him from Comodoro, one that smelled of almonds, or she doesn't remember what. And he didn't let her use it; he'd say that with that Tehuelche hair, it wasn't any use. She should just keep washing her hair with that bar of white soap. That must be when her hair turned blond. Or maybe it was always blond, truth is that even though she just turned forty, she already forgot what color her hair used to be when she was young. The point is, things went on like that, she took care of the house, which she knew a lot about, he sang, and the days went by. They didn't see much of each other because she worked during the day and he at night. There were even times when he would wake her up at three, four in the morning, and tell her to cook something for some woman friend that he'd brought over, an important woman who needed to be treated well. Martina thought they were elegant women, dressed in fancy corsets and silk or fishnet stockings, with dyed hair and lipstick. Women like her, who'd been born out in the country, they didn't wear those kinds of things. She would get up, make them food, then go back to bed because she'd already eaten. One night it took her more time because she felt like making something more complicated, a tripe stew, she thinks, that took longer, so she was up with them for longer. She remembers she had her back turned, working at the kitchen counter, and she heard how they were both laughing, the pop star and the woman who'd come that night. Sometimes both of them laughed and other times, she laughed alone. When it was only her, it was more muted laughter, more childlike, she would say. Heeheehee, she'd go, like a little mouse. The truth is that now that she thinks about it, he was a very optimistic person, he laughed all the time, no matter what was going on. But not even that helps her rid herself of all her hatred for him. They laughed and they drank, he and the woman. The point is, that night Martina took more time with the stew—peeling the vegetables, chopping them up very small, mincing the onions, pulling the strings off the beans, taking the kernels off the corn; these were serious stews, the real deal—and by the time she finished putting everything in the pot, it was about five in the morning. She put the burner on medium, and when she turned around, she saw that there were three empty bottles on the table, and he, her husband, wasn't there. She'd been so focused on the stew, she hadn't noticed that she wasn't hearing them talk anymore. She, the woman who laughed like a little mouse, she was there. She told her that he'd gone to the bathroom, a while ago. She told her that her name was Mariela, but people called her Ángela. It was better for her job. She seemed really nice, even when she wasn't laughing. She smoked, but the lipstick didn't come off. Martina asked her how she did that, because she'd never worn lipstick. The other one took a little mirror out of her shiny purse, and a red lipstick, and showed her how to do it. That first time, Ángela put it on her. When Martina looked at herself in the little mirror, she couldn't believe it. They both starting cracking up.

Martina laughed and looked at herself: her mouth looked like it belonged to somebody else. The kitchen was so warm from the stew that was cooking, and delicious smells started coming out of the pot. Martina thought she'd go ahead and eat twice that night. Even though he wouldn't want her to, she'd take her plate to bed anyway. She'd eat alone, facing the wall, but with lipstick on. The point is, the stew was ready and he still hadn't come out of the bathroom. Martina served two plates for the two of them, so his wouldn't get cold, and heated up some stale bread, and they started to eat. She wondered what things she could talk about with an important woman, what she could say to her. She asked her if she had children. The other said yes, she had a fifteen-year-old daughter, but she lived in Santiago with her grandmother. She started talking about the North, and all the friends she used to have in that small town where she was born. Here in Las Heras, she also had friends, in fact most of her colleagues came from there, but it wasn't the same. For her, when people move they lose something, they change. That's why now she prefers to make friends with people from here, though of course, nobody in Las Heras is from here. Then she told her about the bus she'd taken to come from the North to Santa Cruz. Endless, more than a whole day looking out a filthy window, where actually she couldn't see anything and, deep down, feeling very blue, very little desire to look at anything, to tell the truth. She also told her about the guys she had to put up with every night, the stench of filth in the rooming house where she slept. Then she started up about how lucky she, Martina, was to have a husband and a home. And she started to cry, really sob. Cry and cry. Her eye makeup ran, and she didn't eat the stew; Martina felt like the whole thing was a total failure. And this Ángela woman, with those eyes that looked like black swamps, she made her remember those times when the pop star had gotten a little violent and went at her. Honestly, she didn't know what to do. Martina wanted to cheer her up, do something for Ángela. But she only knew how to do housework, and she'd done that, she'd made a special stew, and even so, the woman didn't stop crying. She ran through her mind, and she couldn't think of anything to say to her, nothing occurred to her. She remembered the times with the magistrate, the policeman, the military man, the garage with all the vials of poison; all in all, nothing seemed right to cheer up anybody. Much less an important woman. Then she remembered. She remembered what the doctor had told her a few days before. She remembered that she had a baby in her belly, and she told her, she told Ángela. She thought that the best thing she could give her would be a secret, something that she hadn't yet told anybody, even if she didn't know if it was good or bad. Nobody else knew it, she was the first to hear; she also told her that. Ángela got quiet for a moment, and Martina thought that she'd really stuck her foot in her mouth, yet again, sometimes the pop star was right when he criticized her. But Ángela asked her for a tissue, and then she kept crying, though this time it was with happiness, she assured her, and she also told her that she wanted to be the baby's godmother. Please, she said to her. It always impressed Martina that she said it the same way she herself speaks to Mother Teresa, as if it were a prayer.

• • •

That child, Ángela's goddaughter, is her oldest daughter, and is a total darling, and has a job as a secretary with Repsol. A princess, just like the other children she had with that good-for-nothing. Amazing how you can have the children of a disgusting human being and still love them to death, as if there weren't a trace of the bad left in them, as if all his ingredients had simply evaporated. It's a good thing, because otherwise they would have turned out as lazy and selfish as the pop star. I am not going to believe it, Martina tells me, when she tells me who finally set her free from that monster. It was her very own mother, the very same one who abandoned her when she was a child. Another monster, true, but at least she served some purpose, for once in her life. Her mother, after she abandoned her when she was a child, did a lot of coming and going, that is, appearing and disappearing from her life. It all depended. If she had herself a new boyfriend, she'd find some hovel and not a peep. But if she was on her own and going through a rough patch, she'd suddenly show up in Martina's life. Especially when the children started coming. That's when she got closer, and she's sure that it's because she really loved them, she liked to watch them grow up, play with them. The attention she never gave her, she did give to the children, even now when they've made her a great-grandmother. The truth is, it's enough to cheer up any woman, even her mother, that's all there is to it. The thing is, when the children started coming, Martina had to get a job to feed so many mouths, so her mother would stay and look after them. And since she was already there, she also started taking care of the pop star, who at that time was less and less pop and less and less a star, and spent most of his time hanging around the house. Sometimes he'd do a gig here or there, but it finally became clear that she, Martina, was the one bringing in the steady income. She doesn't know how it came about, she doesn't know where she found the courage; maybe the kids, necessity, seeing that she couldn't expect much from anybody else around her. The pop star wasn't even bringing women to the house anymore. There he was, pretty much washed up. But she still wanted him around, she wanted her children to always have their father nearby, be able to turn to him if they needed anything. Or not, but to have a father who was somewhere around. And, mostly, that he be their real father. The same father for all four of them. Here in Las Heras, that's no simple feat. People are used to swapping: anybody with anybody. Teenagers with uncles, neighbors with neighbors, doesn't matter. People are very bored, or very confused, she doesn't know which. For example, the other day she heard on the radio an urgent community announcement about a baby who was born with a deformity in her lung, or something like that. The thing is the doctors there at the regional hospital told the mother, a child herself, not even twenty years old, that her baby was terminally ill, that there was nothing they could do, that she should make her peace with it. The baby was a month old, something like that, and that was that, she already had to think about saying goodbye to life. The people at the radio station there in Las Heras always play music and leave some time for community announcements, and that's why between one song and another the announcer talked about the situation and asked if anybody could help to buy a ticket to take the baby to Buenos Aires to see if they could do something there for her. And that's how they got the donations for the ticket, and they saved the baby in Buenos Aires. When they got back to Las Heras, the mother's grandfather was so happy, telling everybody about it, and that's when everybody found out that in addition to being the mother's grandfather he was also the baby's father. And it's fine that she was saved, but she's going to have a little difficulty when she grows up and can't figure out whether to call him daddy or great-grandpa.

But Martina doesn't want to get distracted from the subject of the great-grandmother she was talking about: her own mother. The thing is, after being around the house so much, her mother kind of took over, became kind of like the mistress of the house. A lot goes on when women work so much outside the home. She never liked it, but she'd do anything for her children. Anything and everything. And it's a good thing: now they're angels that make everything more cheerful. The thing is that one day she arrived home, exhausted—at the time, she thinks, she was working at a greengrocers—and found that her husband was in a worse mood than usual. With his band in decline, this was more and more often how he was. And he started a fight with her, telling her that she was raising the children badly, that she was never home, and who knows what other things. And her mother, her very own mother, for the first time in her life, started to defend her. To defend Martina. Her mother: she couldn't believe it. That made her so proud that she almost didn't pay any attention to the things the pop star was throwing at her, or maybe she didn't pay attention because, to tell the truth, she knew that old song and dance and knew that there was nothing new there, and that nothing could be fixed. The point is that her mother started saying that it's not that Martina wasn't raising her kids well but that she had to work so much, that she was carrying the entire burden, and that's why sometimes when she got home, she was tired or distracted, as if she was thinking about other things. Martina tells me this and still clearly feels that wave of joy that she felt when for the first time her mother was her mother. She was on her side. The pop star, who'd drunk even more than usual that day, started attacking her, too, her mother. He said to her—Martina clearly remembers this sentence—you shut up, you're the one who's the happiest about your daughter being out of the house all day. At first Martina thought that she was referring to that issue of her being the mistress of the house, that her mother was happy to have usurped her place, who knows, that can happen when women get old, right? So many things can happen to us when we get old. But, no, it wasn't that at all. It was that the two of them would fuck while Martina was working at the greengrocers. Yup, the pop star and the great-grandmother. When her mother heard that he was coming out with this story, Martina said, she shouted at the top of her lungs, said she was going to sue him, turn him in, kill him, put a Tehuelche curse on him. And of course he didn't flinch. He just started listing the times—when, where they'd been—and as if that weren't enough, he started describing specific details about Martina's mother's body, one by one. That she had a mole on her right ankle, that her left nipple sagged more than the right one, that she had a scar—as if she'd been burned with an iron, he said—on the back of her thigh. He was talking as if he was in front of a jury, making an effort not to forget a single detail that might work in his favor. Martina and her mother looked at him; when he started in on the details, neither was able to say anything. They didn't want to interrupt him: there was something kind of attractive in his very diligent way of remembering a body. Martina says that this was for her what was absolutely unforgivable, what made her decide to leave him forever, even though this meant that her children wouldn't have their father nearby: the attention he'd paid to her mother's body that he'd never paid to hers. He even made it all seem like an act of love. Compared to that, the rest of it was minor: that they fucked, that they spent the time all cozy in bed while she was weighing out bags of potatoes that nobody had taken the mud off of.

It sounds strange, my child, that this is what concerns you, when you've always had less interest in love than in anything.

another excerpt

Martina is tall and slender. She identifies, she says, more with her Tehuelche ancestry, but her appearance is more in line with her German side. The two times we went out on the day we spent together, she wore a short jacket that showed off her narrow waist, despite the authentic sheepskin lining. And she walks with a kind of flexibility, agility, which adds to her elegance. Martina, however, wonders what it is that makes some women attractive to men. She takes for granted that she isn't one of them and instead brings up her mother. She talks about the number of boyfriends her mother has had. Maybe it's a question of attitude, she muses. She remembers how it used to be when all of them were out in the country, during the branding. Because she, in spite of having come here, to Las Heras, she never broke off from the country. She still has some family there, and she always goes to visit. Usually for the branding, which is like a big celebration. There, for example, where there are thousands of men ready to drink and have fun, Martina sees that her mother and some of her sisters are always on high alert. They look at that one, smile at the other, bring a glass of wine to someone over there, laugh at their jokes. In short, they lay out their traps to see what they might catch. Sometimes it's more than two or three during a branding. Sometimes, more than two or three in one night. Her mother, for example, is infallible. Could it be her mole? She, on the other hand, spends those brandings doing something else: looking for the best adversary. Because at those parties that last for days, there's a lot of gambling. Rummy, craps, jacks. She always liked to gamble, and after she separated from the pop star, even more. She doesn't know if it was because he wasn't around any longer to stop her or because her eternal need for money got worse. People tend to see gambling as something reprehensible, perdition, but for her it was a form of sacrifice, a way to feed her children. She looks out of the corner of her eye at Mother Teresa, who in turn keeps looking at us with her arm raised. I, on the other hand, try to never turn to look at that arm. She doesn't know, but she bets that as a child she was good at those games, and once she separated, she became an ace. It was one of the many positive effects of being alone. She remembers those first brandings she went to after she separated as some of the best moments of her life. She's not exaggerating at all. Constant excitement, moments of total happiness. Something was pushing her to play more, to win more. She doesn't really know what it was. Maybe it was the fact of seeing, for the first time, that men were like defenseless little creatures around those smoke-filled tables. She'd take their measure, double down on their bets, and she'd beat them. She'd crush them. Maybe that was it. To sit there and forget everything and at the same time remember everything: her father, the magistrate, the policeman, the military man. And the pop star, above all the pop star. And, after a while, once again, focus only on the winning card, on the number that she had to be able to predict, on the precise moment when she could pull the rug out from under her opponents and leave them flat on their backs. She didn't always get face cards, anyway. Once, out of the blue, she lost a pick-up truck that she'd just managed to win a while before with a series of good hands. She turned over the card and, boom, she lost. Once again, walking around in the cold, taking the kids to school, shivering, hanging onto her. It was the only time she drew such a poisonous card. The only time she really screwed up, that is. Because afterwards she realized that it was something she couldn't allow. If she lost too much she wouldn't have even a few coins to buy milk for the kids. So then she'd appeal to the guys as they were leaving and she'd tell it to them straight. They were from there, from the town, so most of the time they gave her back some of what they'd won from her, at least enough for milk. Other times it wasn't so easy; once there was someone who tried to play the smartass, tried to trade the money that had been hers until just a short time ago for sexual favors, let's say. He said it straight out. She should give him a blow job. On the spot, Martina threw some punches that put his nose out of whack forever, and that dick he wanted to be a smartass with, she left it swollen with a knee to his groin, if not forever then at least for a good long time. The story got out and spread around town. For once she'd managed to teach them to treat her with respect.

> The bull can be master of a thousand cows, if you like, but if he's castrated, he's just a steer surrounded by all those cows.

more of the novel

But of course, when the branding was over, and she had to go back and face her fate as a single woman, separated, mother of four, that's when everything fell apart. Her mother kept helping her at home because in the end you always forgive your mother, but she couldn't give her a cent because she didn't have any herself. Nothing. Then she started to feel exactly like she used to feel as a child when she'd watch the school bus go by from the window of the magistrate's house when she still hadn't finished drying the glasses. It was as if she split into two different people: when she was there, gambling, at the tables, she felt infinitely powerful; but when she had to go back out, look for work, look for a place to live, that's when everything became so difficult again. During that period, right after she'd separated from the pop star, that's when she tried to commit suicide again. She took whatever she could find, but once again they got to her in time. The difference, that time, was that afterwards she swore that it could never happen again. She could never do that again. Now she had four children, and she simply had to eliminate any chance that she would kill herself. During that period, she lived in a garage that she rented from a fat man, behind his house, and sometimes she didn't have the money to pay him. And the fat man was after her, telling her that a blonde like her wasn't born to sleep in a garage but rather in the master bedroom. Yup, the fat man said things that she would have liked someone to say to her and mean it, but she, at that point, knew how to differentiate between a noble feeling and the words of a horny fat man. And, honestly, she couldn't stand it anymore. The children looked at her hands when she got home to see if she'd brought anything to eat, like the dogs out in the country after a slaughter, but she didn't have anything, nothing at all. Just exhaustion. And then there was the fat man. Anyway, that's how it went, she went to an emergency clinic, saying that her stomach really hurt, that she felt like a fire was burning inside her, and when they all turned their backs to see what they could give her to calm her down, she went running to the infirmary, or rather the on-call room, where she'd seen a medicine dispensary on the day she went there to have her youngest son vaccinated, and she grabbed everything she could find. But that was the last time. Seriously. Actually, more than ten years have passed since then.

When she recovered from that final attempt she told herself that what she had to do, if she wanted to make a more or less decent living, was get a man's job. After all, they're the ones who always earn more. So she turned up for a job that was being advertised in a local paper, a position as a mason's assistant. It was a winter morning, she remembers. There was a long line of applicants, because here, in the last few years, if something comes up that isn't related to oil, you've got to jump on it because it will be gone in a flash. She put on her coveralls, thinking that way she would be protected, as a woman. Everybody looked at her, she didn't look at anybody. Luckily, nobody talked to her, until it was her turn to meet the person who was filling out some forms, there at the front of the line. Excuse me, Ma'am, he said to her, but your husband has to come in person to apply for this job. In spite of everything she'd already recounted, Martina's face had never before shown any sign of resentment, but when she repeats that sentence, she flushes, and something sharpens in her eyes. You don't understand, she told him straight. You have absolutely no idea. And she took him, practically by the arm, over to a kind of metal hut that the company had built precariously there for the construction site. She said she wanted to talk to him in private. She explained, without sparing any details, what it was like to be the mother of four children who had a scoundrel for a father and not have anything or anybody else in her life to give her a hand. Nothing and nobody, did he understand? Did he want her to tell him what a woman working as a domestic servant made? Did he want her to tell him what it meant to go back to work as a domestic servant for someone who already at the age of nine had to do that work in order to survive? Did he want her to explain what it meant for a woman to open her legs—in the best-case scenario, because it could also be her mouth or her ass—so that any old washed-up loser could stick it in her? Did he want details about the options that women had or did he prefer to let her do a trial period as a mason's assistant? She'd built countless adobe huts out there in the country; this couldn't be that different. Silent, the guy went silent. He told her that the only condition was that she should always wear those coveralls, and if they could be one size bigger, that would be better, and a hat and goggles. She should hide herself, no-body should find out she was a woman. When they emerged from the shed, the people in line looked at her as if, in fact, she'd opened up one of those aforementioned orifices. They're so imaginative. But what did she care. For a long time now, honestly, men hadn't mattered to her for anything other than beating them at Rummy or craps.

• • •

At that time, precisely when she was more destitute than ever, right then is when she heard news of her father, her father who'd abandoned her before she could even talk and then never showed up again. Never, not a word or a whiff from him. To hear them say, at that moment, when you've hit thirty, have four children, and have racked up a lot more than thirty-four blows, that there's a father out there who is looking for you, it makes your head burst. Honestly, it makes your head burst. He was sick, they told her, terminal, in the hospital in Sarmiento, not far from there. Very sick, and he asked, demanded, to see her. Just what she needed, Martina says. What a lovely life she was dealt. Martina doesn't look at me when she begins with these complaints; she looks at Mother Teresa, as if to find in her a truly worthy female interlocutor. How many times, I think, have they had these conversations. I almost feel like an intruder. Martina didn't even consider going to see him, let him rot there in his hospital bed. Was there anything that connected her to him? Did they have anything to do with each other? Or were they going to come to her with that song and dance about how because one day someone screws someone else, he becomes the father of the baby who had the bad luck to be conceived that day. Let the priests tell those stories to their flocks! The grace of God and all that garbage. A father is someone who takes care of you, protects you, worries about you. She didn't have a father, her precious four children didn't, either. Father in the full meaning of the word. Martina was very resolved, really very resolved that she didn't want anything to do with him, not even to know what kind of disease he had. As far as she was concerned, let him rot very slowly from the inside out while he waited for her, while he stared at the ceiling—because for sure in the hospital in Sarmiento they didn't even have windows to look out of—and waited for her. But it so happened that around that time she met someone very special. Very. A police sergeant, but one who had nothing at all in common with the other one, with the policeman who hired her as a domestic when she was a little girl. Though, to tell the truth, that one wasn't so bad, either, it's just that she doesn't want to remember anything about those years. They make her sick. But this other one was so handsome, with that uniform and those strong legs. He was a looker. And so sweet, so understanding. A creature from another world. Sometimes she'd lie down and he'd stroke her head, and she'd feel that the weight of the world had lightened, that there were moments in life when you could stand up and others when you could rest because another human being could do something for you. He'd just stroke her head, that's all, and it was as if everything changed its weight, its color. Martina thought it was incredible, like being on drugs. With him she also felt what it was to be a woman. An orgasm, she means. The first in her life. She still remembers that day they went out for a drive in the country. That's common around here: people go out of town, and stop somewhere and well, things happen that are supposed to happen. In this case, she wondered what would happen. It had been about ten years since she'd separated from the pop star, and since then she'd had nothing to do with men. She had so much going on with the children, who were growing up so well and were so demanding at the same time, that honestly she couldn't think about anything else. At that time she was no longer working as a mason's assistant, even though it had turned out to be a fantastic job, which had lasted about five years. She'd ended up being very close friends with all her coworkers, and of course right away they figured out that she was a woman, and they asked her only one favor: that Martina would always go to work in the coveralls and goggles because if their wives ever found out that they spent the entire day with a two-meter-tall blonde, they'd kill them. That's how they described her, she tells me, what do you think? A two-meter-tall blond. She made good friends from that period, very good people. Honestly, now she's just grateful that things have changed so much. She has this loving husband, who keeps her company, she has her children, who've made her a grandmother. But, as she was saying, that man, that police sergeant, he was for her a before and an after. She's not saying this because of the orgasm, she clarifies, which definitely is a lovely sensation, but riding a horse out in the country is also a lovely sensation or getting up early in the morning and drinking maté alone, without anybody talking to you. It's not the sensation but rather the consequences: she felt that for the first time she had a right, a right to have a good time with another person, something she thought only happened to men. Women were supposed to be like a receptacle for them to have a good time in, but not participants. He was the one, because of how good he made her feel, because of the love that he showed her, who convinced her to go see her father. If it hadn't been for him, for the sergeant, she never would have gone. But he said something very important; he didn't say that she should go to be kind or any of that nonsense that her friends would have said if she'd had any or her mother would have said if she weren't so stupid and selfish. He told her that she should do it out of curiosity, to see his face, how he spoke, to see why she was so blonde and so tall when she kept saying she was Tehuelche. What a dear man, Martina says, and turns to look back at Mother Teresa. It lasted such a short time. Two months later they killed him, a bullet to his forehead, right between the eyes. He was chasing a thief and: Bam! Dead in a flash. That's how it went, that's how it went and how it ended. But she learned so much from him. To this day she is still grateful to Mother Teresa that she met him, even though she then had to take him away. She knows; she understands. The following week, when she'd recovered a little, she went to leave flowers on his grave, and then, directly from there, she went to the hospital to see her father. She felt she had to do it for him, for the sergeant. He was so convinced that it was the best thing for her, that Martina took it as an implicit promise, like something that had been communicated from mind to mind on one of those days when he was stroking her head. Because honestly, when it came to curiosity, she didn't have any.

A woman wearing a white coat standing at the entrance to the hospital pointed her down a corridor, then said that she should turn down another, and finally she mentioned a third door she had to enter. All that while giving signals to someone up on a ladder, changing some light bulbs, she thinks. Better for her. For Martina, asking for the room of Mr. F. had made her very uncomfortable, as if she couldn't say her own last name in reference to anybody other than herself. She knocked on the door to the room and nobody answered. She pushed on it gently, carefully, as if it were made of cardboard, and she saw that there were three parallel beds in a room painted white, or that had been painted white at some point. And, just as she thought, it didn't have windows. In one of the beds was a woman who was fast asleep, probably drugged. In the other two were men. One of them looked at her and smiled. She eked out a smile but didn't feel like opening her mouth. He was in pretty good shape, about sixty years old, sitting up, leaning against a pile of pillows, reading a newspaper. He looked healthy; that must not be her father. The other, the third person in the room, was lying down, his back to the door, facing the wall. Martina had no way of knowing if he was sleeping or not. She couldn't see if the blankets were moving to the rhythm of some kind of respiration. That was her father, and she had the good luck of arriving just moments after he died. The way these weird coincidences happen when someone dies. She always remembered a woman who'd told her about when her father died, also in a hospital bed, how the clock that he'd always had hanging on the wall in the dining room, that he'd brought from Seville, stopped at exactly the same moment he took his last breath. Exactly.

Martina stood there, but nothing changed around her. The man reading the newspaper, who was the only one who could say something, was definitely interested in the news. It seemed like it wasn't just that he'd grabbed it to pass the time, to wait for some relative or nurse to talk to. She couldn't count on him. She tells me now that at that moment she already knew that her father was the one on the right, the one looking at the wall. She doesn't know how that kind of certainty gets stuck in the mind, but she has proof that it does. She took a couple of steps toward that bed. She saw that he was well covered; it would have made her terribly uncomfortable to see her father half dressed, wearing those white underpants old men wear and that sometimes they forget to close up. She stretched out her head and saw that the man—her father, let's say, she tells me—wasn't asleep: his eyes were open, staring at the wall. She was about to run out, she had the urge. She cursed herself for going alone, but the truth is that it seemed cruel to bring her children to witness such a thing. She would have brought her mother, but she refused, she said she had absolutely no desire to see that piece of filth again. From the side she saw that her nose, Martina's, long and with a sharp point at the end, was the same as this man's. She tried to remember the last time she'd seen him, but she didn't have a single memory. According to her calculations, she was three years old when he left, because it happened at least a couple of years before her mother left. She hadn't been able to recall a single physical feature. To have to come here now, she thought, with everything she had to do, to waste time thinking about these things that had happened so long ago. Let bygones be bygones. But she remembered her sergeant, her promise to him. She cleared her throat, but the man didn't react. What should she call him? Papá? Mr. F.? She could hear some sounds coming from other rooms; someone let out a piercing scream. Not even this made him react, this supposed father. She approached and touched his arm. She preferred to do even this than address him in some specific way. Then he did turn. He looked at her the way he looked at the wall, only half there. I'm Martina, she said, the one you asked them to call. When he turned she saw that his face was boney, large, and when she spoke to him a grimace of pain rippled through his features. She saw that he didn't even have a nightstand next to his bed, a place to put his things. Didn't matter, she hadn't brought anything. They spoke only the bare minimum. She didn't try to sit down because that would have meant sitting on the bed he was in. There wasn't a chair nearby, either. He told her he had terminal cancer and that she was the only daughter he'd ever had. When he spoke his features didn't soften. She told him that she had four children and that she hated him.

TEN

Because you have to live in a daze to know what it's like, what it feels like. A daze: overwhelmed by the stories that take over your head, try to control your thoughts, your willpower. Voices that don't give you a moment's peace. Sandra paces around her kitchen as she talks. Voices that fill your head with stories, she says, as she shakes her youthful bangs that match the cast of her face though not her age. Her head is small, scrawny, as if the stories were Jivaros, shrinking her head a little more each day.

And there are so many other stories they cram into her head. The story "Black Pots," for example, which has a creepy parricidal character; or "Boa-ua-ie," the story of a nine-year-old boy; or there's that story about the old tramp. They're like the stories in the *Thousand and One Nights*: they go on and on, they never end. She spelled them all out clearly in the letter she wrote to the director of the National Lottery. It was published in the newspaper, the whole thing. The local newspaper, in Las Heras, but also the one in Comodoro. People even came from the national news agency, Telam, to interview her. It's all spelled out there. It says clearly who the people are who focus their attention and broadcast those stories so they can take over the minds of the inhabitants of Las Heras. Who they are and why they're doing it. She's going to report all of them, she's got piles of evidence. And she's not talking here about something trivial. She's talking about an extremely powerful sect, one of the most powerful in the world. There are seven of them, she's identified them all. They're the owners of the town's Lottery House. Seven of them, the whole family. From the old lady to the youngest, who's twelve years old. He's the worst, Sandra is convinced. A true incarnation of the Devil. All of them, all seven, focus their attention in one bed. All night. Sometimes all night and all day. That's why the old woman who works at the shop attached to the Lottery House always looks so haggard, so tired. Lurking there behind the candy display, with those eyes like black garbage bags. Like those *Media Hora* hard candies they tortured us with when we were kids: black balls, that's her eyes. She's not a good person who's just tired of her job. No, Sandra knows it's about something else, or at least about another kind of job. She hears them, they put her in a daze. They don't leave her alone, by day or by night.

Sandra knows it's them, the whole family, who focus their attention at night and insinuate themselves into the dreams of people in Las Heras. The dreams of the Lashereños. That's how they operate: they focus, they're like a sect, they stick those stories into people's heads and from then on, they don't stop, they fill their heads and they don't stop. They don't stop until the story, through its dream clues, reveals the winning number. You've got to know all about it. You've got to know how to implant those stories into dreams and you have to know how to decode them. They know, because they've taken classes in mind control and because they belong to the most powerful sect in the world. Not the most powerful, the second most powerful. But that's still something. When people dream those stories, they focus all their attention, go inside, and get the winning number. Because those stories always transmit a number, always, inevitably. In those stories, in code, is the winning number. They're evildoers. Once they have those numbers, they play them themselves. Even though they have their Lottery House, that's got nothing to do with it. They play them somewhere else, so that nobody catches them; they get the numbers at night, when the poor Lashereños are trying to sleep, and the next day they play them in Pico Truncado, in Río Gallegos. That's why she's asking the Lottery authorities to investigate, because then they'll see the amount of winning numbers this group has managed to amass.

Merging the draws was difficult; but we must remember that the individuals of the Company were (and are) all-powerful and astute. In many cases, the knowledge that some good luck was simply the result of chance would have diminished their virtue; in order to avoid this inconvenience, the Company agents employed the power of suggestion and magic. The steps they took, their manipulations, were carried out in secret. In order to probe the private hopes and private terrors of every person, they deployed astrologists and spies . . . The drunkard who extemporizes an absurd mandate, the dreamer who suddenly awakes, strangling with his own hands the woman sleeping next to him, aren't they also carrying out the Company's secret decisions? Such silent workings, comparable to God's, lead to all sorts of speculations.

from "The Babylonian Lottery" by Jorge Luis Borges

That's how they've gotten rich, Sandra says, by consuming people's minds. Constantly implanting stories. And not everybody in Las Heras reacts in the same way, of course. But everybody displays, in their own way, the signs of destruction. The total destruction that controls this town, and looks like the spawn of the Devil himself. The stories, no matter how they play out, ultimately lead to destruction. For example, there are cases of people who are slowly persuaded to abandon everything, and they end up on the streets. Like what happened to this man, she says, and she points to a jacket that hangs on the back of one of her kitchen chairs. That man was a normal person, a good father, with a house, a job. And now what? Now he's a tramp, and poor bum who lives on the streets. All he's got are two scrawny dogs who follow him around. And this jacket, which Sandra promised to mend for him. She shows me the inside: through the shredded lining can be seen the matted stuffing, fake sheepskin. The jacket seems to me to be beyond repair, but Sandra shows me the section where she's planning to cut the fabric so she can patch some of the holes. Like surgeons do, when they take skin off the thigh and use it on the throat. The case of the tramp, Sandra continues, is typical. A typical victim of the sect of the seven. Then there are other cases, people who are even less able to resist the stories in their heads, and they're the ones who simply kill themselves, mostly teenagers and children. Obviously, they have less ability to resist the stories from taking over their heads, heads that are still fresh, that don't have as many defenses.

> In Las Heras, between 1996 and the end of 1999, sixteen people between the ages of eighteen and thirty committed suicide, as well as one older person. We should also add, to date—January 2003—three additional suicides, including two minors, that took place in December 2000 and in December 2002, and the suicide of a person between forty and fifty years old, in the local jail. The last one, in December 2002, was the youngest suicide, at twelve years old. We must also consider the high number of suicides prevented or attempted suicides that are never recorded. Data obtained from community sources attest to numerous cases.
>
> *from "A Socioeconomic Analysis of Las Heras," by Antonio Grant,*
> *Las Heras Department of Social Advocacy*

The children of Las Heras hang themselves. To the statistics cited in the report must be added the eight suicides and the eight attempted suicides during the rest of 2003, the year with the highest rate since it all began, 1999. Sandra says that the method they choose to kill themselves supports her theory, for those prompted by these kinds of cults always opt for a rope around their necks. It occurs to me, though of course I don't dare contradict her, that this is the easiest, most accessible, method. Here, in the middle of this desert, there's nowhere to drown yourself, no bridge to jump off, no tall buildings. No pharmaceuticals within reach, like in big cities. Maybe they're all afraid that the pharmacist will go around telling people what they're taking. Pills and the entire metaphor of healing they evoke seem out of place in this town that, until the appearance of oil in the thirties—even though they didn't really begin pumping until the end of the fifties—was quite rural in its idiosyncrasies. If they're going to swallow something, they tend to go for insecticides or, as happened once, water with crushed glass. Then there are weapons, but young people don't usually use them. It's not a matter of money: you can buy them cheaply and easily on the black market. Maybe it's because killing yourself with a weapon implies excessive violence: more blood, more noise; more responsibility because there's a choice—to aim for the head or the heart—or more margin for error. At the hospital they say that many of the unsuccessful suicide attempts were with a weapon, either a gun or a knife. In addition, those young people turn all the violence against themselves. Wholesale. In Las Heras, you don't see what happens in other places, where a child comes to school with a machine gun and massacres their entire class. In spite of the suppressed violence that you breathe in this town, that reflex to turn it on others doesn't exist. Perhaps that's the most unnerving thing about this place, these children: they don't blame or victimize others. One day, they simply tie a rope around their necks and jump. From a bench, from a bed, from the kitchen table. Nobody suspected anything the day before; nobody manages to explain it on the days that follow. While the townspeople who are no longer teenagers propose a series of theories to explain these deaths—90 percent of whom cite supernatural factors—

young people offer nothing but random, truncated phrases. They sound like haikus of horror.

• • •

I walk through the town's main square and approach a group of five young people sitting in a circle in the front yard of an abandoned house across the street. The house has become notorious in town for several reasons: that's where they meet to do their deals or smoke their joints in peace—some would say it serves the same function as a gentlemen's club—and there, also, against the backdrop of its mustard façade, someone wrote in graffiti, "Las Heras: Pueblo Fantasma." Las Heras: Ghost Town. A journalist from Buenos Aires who visited Las Heras at the end of 2001—when the city, UNICEF, and the Foundation for Citizen's Power met to try to implement a nonviolent conflict resolution program managed by Harvard University—quoted those words in the first paragraph of his article. The young people say that a lot of old people are offended by the way that article portrayed the town, but for them it's true, it's a ghost town. They are constantly changing the subject. Yes, of course they knew the people who killed themselves. No idea; absolutely no idea why they did it. It's cold here, all year, they say. I recall what Nick Nolte says in *Nightwatch*, the movie in which a night caretaker at the morgue becomes a suspect in a series of murders: there's not always an explanation that brings closure. The well-documented and credible hows and whys are assembled for the families that suffer, and for the screenwriters of detective shows. But when you really want to get to the bottom of it, the whole story falls apart, there are gaps, unknowns, a senselessness that is better to make friends with. That's more or less what Nick Nolte says in *Nightwatch*.

LAS HE_A S
PUE__O fA___AJŊA

Marcos hung himself with a striped plastic hose that he slung over a beam in one of the half-built houses across the street from his house. Right across the street. His mother, Zulema, talks about what happened and points, from her window, to the sites of the drama: there, in that room on the left, is where he hung himself; there, from that ceiling beam; there, in that empty lot, is where they always used to play. He—twelve years old when he died—and his three younger sisters, who are now circling around the kitchen like lost ghosts, squeezing through the gap between the two chairs where their mother and I are sitting. They pass by, look, say nothing. *I see dead people*: they look like those ghostly characters that poor kid in *The Sixth Sense* would glimpse. They didn't always play all together because it hadn't been that long since Marcos had come to live with his mother. Before, he lived with his father, who'd been in prison for prostituting minors. A neighbor girl from around the corner. The mother of the girl was also charged as an accomplice. Zulema is from a Tehuelche community called Limonao. Precisely now, right when she started night school, this happens.

I cross the street to the abandoned house and the younger siblings follow me like automatons, as if it were simply a matter of going to the place where they always play. The walls of the room where Marcos hung himself are completely covered in black lettering written with charcoal. It's a *cumbia villera*, a slum cumbia, the tallest of the little brothers tells me, and that's when I hear his voice for the first time. "His friends and his family will visit him today / two months for stealing he's already paid / he fell madly in love without ever seeing / that slowly his life would be crashing and crumbling / White and pure was the mistress who controlled his life / That's when he knew madness, that's when he finally lost control / et cetera."

The handwriting is nimble, determined, the handwriting of someone who has a daily relationship with the written word. Marcos came here with his three younger siblings, told them to help him hang the hose there to play a new game, climbed onto a couple of boxes that he'd managed to find in the neighborhood, one on top of the other, and jumped. His siblings watched him spinning around up there in circles, withdrawn, and they wondered what the point was of setting up a game that in the end only one person can play.

• • •

In the hotel that night, lying on a bed two centimeters smaller than the room itself, I can't fall asleep. I think about the novel that I read when I must have been about ten, twelve years old, *The Stepford Wives*, by Ira Levin, who also wrote *Rosemary's Baby*. It takes place in one of those towns in the United States where everything seems to be okay: the houses with their curtains, the children with their cereals, and the couples with their anniversary parties. At a certain point, everything slowly starts to be *too* good. The patterns on the curtains become more and more sophisticated, as do the anniversary parties, and the women's traits, those traditionally associated with femininity, become accentuated. They begin to prepare more elaborate dishes, they converse with their women friends only about domestic subjects, they smile affectionately at their husbands when they come home from work, and their tits and asses get rounder. The women turn into caricatures of themselves. I think it was told from the point of view of the last woman who's about to fall into those rituals, and that was what always made such an impression on me: her in-depth story about the strangeness that slowly takes over everything that until then had been familiar to her. This woman begins to realize that the men of Stepford have formed a kind of cult, whose mission is to remove the human aspects of women and turn them into robotic guardians of the home, eternally smiling. They were all men who, before moving to Stepford, had been married to successful women. They had not, it seems, been entirely comfortable in that role, and that's why they eagerly participated in the fantasy of keeping them under control. A little like the plan that Jeffrey Dahmer, the Butcher of Milwaukee, wanted to perfect, though in this case the experiment is a success. By the time the last Stepford wife figures things out, the mission is far advanced: she has remained alone in that town of puppets. In 2004, Frank Oz made a film version of this novel, which he managed to completely ruin. It stars Nicole Kidman, the tone is comedic and lacks any and all charm, the script neither freed itself from nor captured Levin's story, and the sense that it's a satire of the feminist struggle looms over it. For me, on the contrary, that story will always be one of "psychological terror," to use the marketing language of the movie industry. The slow extermination of a species. I think that's why I recall it tonight, because something similar seems to be happening here, in Las Heras, with the youth. If they don't commit suicide, they find other ways of canceling themselves out, of turning themselves into puppets: they consume substances that stupefy them for life, and they get pregnant in order to be diluted with another.

> A darkly brilliant tale of modern devilry that induces the reader to believe the unbelievable. I believed it and was altogether enthralled.
>
> *Truman Capote on* Rosemary's Baby

Those kids were victims of witches' apprentices. The poor women have to practice on somebody. That's why they start with the easiest ones: teenage souls are always so weak, so vulnerable to influence. You have to learn how to do something as difficult as taking over a person's will, another person's mind. And here in Las Heras it happens a lot. The desire to control, to take over another person's fate. They do it through salaries and through minds. The truth is, that's why Miguel left here a few years ago; he woke up one morning and realized that he couldn't stand it any longer. At least three times a week, someone would come and ask him to do something to someone else: to destroy their marriage, their business, ruin them. Always negative things, of course. Who's going to go through all that bother to do something good? We do good things ourselves, it's rare for someone to delegate a good deed to someone else. Everybody, deep down, spends their life accumulating Credits and Debits. That's one of the problems with his vocation: they hire him so that the Debit always belongs to somebody else. That's why he left; now he comes into Las Heras only every once in a while. Two, three days at most. And he tries to be as inconspicuous as possible; truth is, after living in this town for five years, he can barely say he still has a couple of friends. He sees them and then returns to Los Antiguos, where his family and a group of disciples are waiting for him. This whole Patagonia business is relatively new for him; he used to wander around the world, learning everything he now knows. Spain, India, Thailand. All the techniques that help him do healing, because the truth is that's what it's about for him. But here in Las Heras nobody wanted to understand him. Nobody. People never even came to ask for a massage. Always something against other people, something hurtful. He has to admit that he's never seen a society so preoccupied with others, honestly.

The community of Las Heras right now is in shock. To deny it, to ignore this reality, to not make an attempt to write about what's happening to us, would not be okay. At least that's what I think. What is really going on?

from an editorial in the weekly La Ciudad, *Las Heras, September 1999*

There was a big uproar. A mistake, a real mistake. Father Augusto was the parish priest when the chain of suicides began. Not anymore, he doesn't live in Las Heras anymore. He left after his heart surgery, that's when he asked for a transfer to another town somewhere else. Now couples come see him to ask for advice because they're leaving for the North, following their children and grandchildren; somewhere not like Las Heras at all. He remembers the first kid: he knew his family. The aunt who'd raised him. It's inexplicable. A kid with so much potential, who was finishing high school and getting ready to go to the university. There are so many problematic kids there, young people who don't know what to do, hanging out in the square, taking anything they can get their hands on, girls pregnant at fifteen, but the whole thing that started with the chain of suicides, if we want to call it that, is a whole other story. Life is full of mysteries. A kid with a girlfriend who loved him. It was wrong, wrong, wrong to hold the wake at school. School is an environment designed for education, not death. Those freezing cold classrooms. All because the aunt is the principal. Not of that one, another one, a grammar school, but anyway a principal. It's understandable that in the middle of all that sorrow the woman would want to seek out an environment that would be close, intimate, some venue where she could feel minimally whole. But it was a mistake; she turned the whole thing into a spectacle. And it's well known what teenagers will do to get attention. Anything. Especially those teenagers, who have so many unmet needs. Absent fathers, who work fourteen hours a day in the oil wells. Or straight out nonexistent fathers, fathers who never knew they were fathers. Self-sacrificing mothers, who transmit to them that quotient of neglect and resentment where nothing can prosper. Or wayward mothers, forever trapped in that same feeling of neglect. All of those kids, it's like they've mutated and don't know where they're headed or why. In short, a complicated picture. And on top of that, when something happens, they all make such a fuss. A mistake, he never tires of repeating. The priest thinks that the media contributed a lot; they put on their own spectacle in order to sell more papers, when they should have kept quiet. In fact, he has just read a book that describes what happened somewhere in the United States where there was also a spate of suicides among young people, a chain reaction. In the middle of that process, it seems, the wave stopped: there wasn't a single death for a whole month. People actually took deep breaths, cautiously, afraid of changing this microclimate where a certain calm seemed to have set settled in. After some time—a long time after the suicides inevitably started up again—they realized, the priest says the book says, that the interval when there was a break in the chain had coincided with a newspaper strike.

CONMOCION Y DESCONCIERTO

El enigma de no saber qué hacer

La comunidad de Las Heras está por estas horas conmovida. Negarlo. Dejar pasar esta realidad. No tratar de escribir algo sobre lo que nos pasa no estaría bien. Al menos es lo que yo opino. Qué es lo que está pasando? Qué m.... les pasa a los jóvenes? Qué nos pasa? Por qué todos los lashereños de un tiempo a esta parte tenemos que vivir con el corazón en la boca cuando nos llegan estas noticias infaustas que no tienen una explicación lógica? Todo en la vida tiene un sentido. Todo se hace siguiendo una dirección. Todos tenemos objetivos –distintos- es cierto, pero apostando siempre a lo que vendrá porque es lo que nos mantiene vivos. Pero qué les está pasando, muchachos? No tienen sueños, no tienen ilusiones, no tienen en quién pensar? Por qué no toman conciencia de lo duro que se está poniendo vivir y ustedes lo solucionan todo en un instante fatal? Por qué son tan egoístas y piensan nada más que en ustedes, en cómo evadirse de los problemas si es que realmente los tienen? Por qué actúan con tanto ego y deciden ustedes el sufrimiento eterno de quienes quedan llorándolos? Es que no piensan en sus seres queridos, es que no piensan en que la vida es más linda y tiene más sentido cuando aparecen los desafíos? Es que no tienen a nadie en este mundo superpoblado de gente para que simplemente los escuche? Me gustaría tener la verdad absoluta y saber cuál es la causa de todo esto que está sucediendo en nuestra localidad. Hablan de males, de demonios, de problemas laborales, sentimentales o financieros. De listas, de sectas. De que es una modalidad que están siguiendo los jóvenes. ¡¡¡Paren la mano que no es joda!!!, ¿de qué están hablando? NADA es tan grave como pasar en un instante a NO SER NADA. No hay nada que justifique esta sucesión de hechos trágicos que lastiman, que dañan, que duelen, que nos dejan a todos los que habitamos este suelo con una preocupación mayor a la que tenemos por el simple hecho de levantarnos cada mañana, pelearle a la vida todos los días y tratar de ir solucionando los problemas que se nos presentan.

Porque de eso se trata. ¿O es que la quieren toda fácil?

Peleen, luchen, busquenle la vuelta, busquen un motivo para VIVIR, AUNQUE SEA UNO SOLO y ¡¡¡¡metanle masa!!!!, como bien les gusta decir a ustedes.

Todos los lashereños estamos hoy preocupados, escandalizados, alarmados y coincidimos por primera vez en mucho tiempo TODOS de que tenemos que hacer algo y que esto no puede seguir así...

Pero la pregunta es:

¿Qué hacer? ..., ¿cómo evitar esto?....., ¿a quién hay que recurrir?...., ¿qué es lo que debemos decirle a los jóvenes?...

Afortunadamente parte de la comunidad local se ha sentido tocada y se vislumbran para el futuro medidas de asistencia solidaria.

Ojalá que todo lo que se haga sirva para algo y que esto que actualmente vivimos en nuestra localidad pase a formar parte de la historia negra que deberá quedar en el olvido.

Es lo que esperamos TODOS los lashereños, unidos en una desgracia colectiva sin igual que deberemos desterrar definitivamente.

SHAKEN AND CONFUSED

The conundrum of not knowing what to do

The community of Las Heras right now is in shock. To deny it, to ignore this reality, to not make an attempt to write about what's happening to us, would not be okay. At least that's what I think.

What is really going on?

What the H— is going on with our youth? What's going on with us? Why, for some time now, have all us Lashareños had to live with our hearts in our mouths when we hear so much troubling news that has no logical explanation?

Everything in life has some meaning.

Everything that happens follows some order.

We all have goals, different ones it's true, but we always wager on what the future holds because that's what keeps us alive.

But what's going on with you, kids?

Don't you have any dreams, any illusions, don't you have anything to think about?

Why, when you realize how hard life is getting, do you think you can solve everything in one fatal moment?

Why are you so selfish and think only about yourselves, about how to avoid problems, if you really have any?

Why do you act so selfishly and condemn those you leave behind, those who mourn you, to eternal suffering?

Don't you think about your loved ones, don't you think that life is beautiful and has even more meaning when challenges arise?

Don't you have anybody in this overpopulated world who can listen to you?

I'd love to know the whole truth and know the cause of everything that's happening in our town.

There's talk about curses, devils, problems with work, love, money. About lists, about sects. That it's a fad young people are following.

Stop! This isn't a joke!!!! What are they talking about???

NOTHING is as serious as NOT BEING

ANYTHING in a split second.

There is nothing that justifies this series of tragic events that wound, that hurt, that are painful, that leave all of us who live in this region with an even bigger worry than the one we have from the simple fact of waking up every morning, struggling with life every day, and trying to deal with problems as they arise.

Because that's what it's about. Or do you want everything to be easy?

Struggle, fight, find solutions, find a reason to LIVE, EVEN IF YOU CAN ONLY FIND ONE!!! Dig in, as you yourselves like to say!!

All of us Lashereños are worried, outraged, alarmed, and we all agree for the first time in a long time that we ALL have to do something and that this cannot go on like this . . .

But the question is:

What should we do . . . ? How can we prevent this . . . ? To whom can we turn . . . ? What should we tell our youth . . . ?

Fortunately, some in our local community have risen to the occasion and propose measures of mutual aid for the future. Hopefully it will all have some effect, and what is going on now will become part of the dark history that should be consigned to oblivion.

That is what ALL Lashareños hope for, united in an unprecedented collective misfortune that must be definitively rooted out.

editorial in No. 209 of local weekly La Ciudad, *September 1999*

Nobody. Germán knows very well what it is like to have nobody to talk to. Nobody that answers you, in other words, because if he wants to talk, he can talk to the dogs and cats he lives with. There are twenty in all. Each one with its own problems: it's a struggle. He just moved houses, and you should see how they're doing, the poor things. They're in crisis, a crisis of place, belonging. These days Germán is trying not to go out much so he can be with them through their adjustment process. But it's not easy, not for him, either. They all went from living in a big, beautiful house to this one, where things are different: it's small, the bathroom is outside, the walls are unpainted stucco. And all because he couldn't afford the rent in the other place. That's why he, Germán, cries so much. If someone, anyone, knew how much he cries. He lent money to another teacher who works with him there, at the school, and his colleague never paid him back. She couldn't. She asked for it to get a loan and buy a house, the other teacher did, and then she couldn't pay it back. He doesn't know, honestly he doesn't know what he would do without them, his pets, who help him cope with so much humanity. So much. Or without his poetry, which gushes out of him. Lately there's not a single day that he doesn't return home crying, drowning in tears, as they say. How he cries, what a way to cry. Seriously, so many things going on. And he's had to deal with difficulties ever since he was young, forever. His father who drank, his mother, who knows where she was. He had to be raised by his grandmother, because both of them were always off doing their thing, each on his or her own. By the time he was a teenager, he was a mess. Forsaken by God, right here in this town. And gay, definitely gay. Having to deal with it. Here, in Las Heras. He fled when he was a teenager. Later, he didn't, later he returned and now he's here. He'll never leave this place. The others have even gotten used to the idea that this man with an orange shock of hair and flowing, flamboyant garments is their children's teacher. They're even grateful to have someone who loves them as if they were his own children. Even more, Germán loves those kids a lot more than many of their own parents love them, there's absolutely no doubt about that. Those poor lost kids, they're like drowning chicks. He teaches them, but that's not all: he also organizes poetry contests, cultural events, athletic events. Here, if the school doesn't support them, nobody does. And they're the first ones to acknowledge it; they might skip class, for example, but they don't leave school; on the contrary, they might stay to smoke a joint in the courtyard, sleep in a hallway. It's the closest thing they have to a home, that is, it's the place they find what they don't have at home. Germán knows all about it. About not having anything. How dare they blame these poor creatures, as if it were their decision to feel like life is a piece of shit somebody forced them to stick their noses into and smell and smell. As if it were their decision. They blame them, hurl accusations at them. He knows all about that. When he got the hell of out of Las Heras at the end of the seventies, beautiful years, he was even out on the streets, eating whatever he could find. They're going to come tell him what it is to feel like the last rat to leave the ship. To wake up in the middle of the night with an empty stomach, starving and freezing to death, nothing but despair around you. Existence, like a vacuum cleaner that sucks you in, sucks you in, while telling you: you are garbage and, because you are garbage, you have to be part of my little bag of dirt. Come, let me suck you up. That's why he went North, at least there he'd be out of the cold. At that time he worked for a politician from Tucumán. He was a kind of valet. The things he had to do there, at those parties. Better not to go into too many details. One day he decided to return. Here, to Las Heras. He doesn't really know why, what he does know is that he will never leave here, never. He has something to do in this town, something to do for these kids. And then there are his pets, of course, who would have a hard time getting used to a different place. They're from here, like he is.

The official coat of arms of the city of Las Heras is divided into three sections. The top section shows a clear blue sky and a transparent white cloud, which represents a vent of gas, one of our region's most abundant resources. The background colors, mostly yellow and red, represent the Patagonian dawn; the dark beige, black, and white correspond to the dominant colors of the meseta.

The interpretation of the symbols that comprise the coat of arms speaks clearly to the spirit that animates the inhabitants of a region abundant in elements that guarantee its future. Against the background of a Patagonia permanently swept clean by our southerly winds is an arrowhead that represents the noble race that, for the last ten thousand years, has inhabited the region; along with it, and representing the social, temporal, and cultural evolution of the people of the region, an oil well emphasizes the production of black gold.

Finally, the most ancient child of these lands, the

guanaco, indomitable and proud, next to the meekness of the sheep, mainstays to man's survival in the South. The name of the town and the province on a blue and white stripe speaks to national integration.

description of the official coat of arms of Las Heras, designed by Saúl O. Melián, winner of the competition held in 1978.

"Las Heras was not founded, it rose through its own gravitational pull," says the first line of a fascicule that I found in the local library. There is no book about it: the history of Las Heras has to be read like that, in fascicules, newspaper cuttings, pamphlets, official documents, fragments. As the opening sentences of an origin story, "Las Heras was not founded," does not appear to portend anything good. The town arose when what was meant to be a major project came to halt: the Trans-Patagonia Railway that would unite Puerto Deseado with the Andes Mountains, and, in the future, with the Pacific Ocean. It became, literally, the end of the line. It was 1914, the First World War had begun, and with it, a shortage of iron. After they'd laid a little more than two hundred kilometers of rail, the entire project was abandoned. Right here. The lack of iron explains the failure, in part. Another big part is explained in the book by Bailey Willis, the North American geologist who initiated the research for the route of the Trans-Patagonia Railway; in it is described in detail the vernacular bureaucracy and corruption Willis had to deal with as he attempted to carry out projects that were ultimately abandoned, such as this railway. *A Yanqui in Patagonia: A Bit of Autobiography*, published by Stanford University Press in 1947, under a title that Willis really didn't deserve, can be read as an account of or as notes for a treatise about the causes of our national failure.

• • •

The track that Willis helped plan can still be seen as you exit the bus station. In 1914, the men who were advancing toward the Andes were left stranded here, in this exact spot. They waited. First for some news, then for a decision. Shutting down a project can take as much time as starting one up, though the opposite is usually claimed. The men had been prepared to spend years on this, they had dropped everything in order to work on this project for the long term, and suddenly they found themselves here and didn't know what to do. No reaction. It's understandable. In addition to the paralysis often provoked by these abrupt endings—as with a death or unexpected news—one must add, in their case, the hypnosis produced by this meseta. I think it comes from a combination of the apparent monotony of the landscape, the constant wind, and the brutal presence of the sky. It's a combination of factors that has taken me years to define, and I still have my doubts. These men stayed here, under that effect, and without anything to do. For them, it was the end of the line. They had already spent about five years preparing the terrain, laying the track from Puerto Deseado, until one day the supplies, the money, the foremen, and the orders stopped showing up. There was a kind of breakdown, and disorientation ensued. They were all left like a static image, slightly out of focus. Or like those frozen corpses that someone finds on the slopes of Everest, held for who knows how many years with that expression on their faces that never planned on being the last. There was not, on the other hand, a place to return to. Or, better said, what to return to. To wait, in these cases, is always a refuge. Even an act of optimism. Until maybe something happens. The men prepared a place where they could settle in, and, with time, some arranged to work as cart drivers, taking advantage of being right smack in the middle between the mountains and the sea, to drive carts loaded with wool and hides. They would do with carts what the train was going to do. Others joined together to build a hotel. "El Progreso," they called it. That's how Las Heras ended up where it ended up: smack in the middle, at the midpoint between the sea and the mountains. On the dreaded meseta. Everything is the same color, somewhere between white and yellow. Anything green that grows here can claim to be a miracle.

At first, the town was called El Rastro del Avestruz, The Track of the Ostrich. Would things have turned out the same, I wonder, if someone had done something to prevent them from changing the name to Las Heras?

• • •

It's because of that, the aridity, that Sandra's job, tending the gardens of YPF managers, is so difficult. What would, somewhere else, be the indifferent workings of nature, here is a clash of the Titans, a permanent struggle between conflicting forces. Each one of those houses that sits on the edge of town facing the meseta is, with its little front garden, a kind of battle station, a fort where good is shown to always triumph over evil. Like in those drawings we used to make in school, there's the picket fence, the little path that passes through a couple of meters of green leading to the front door, a rose bush, a tree, one that is forever dwarfed. And across the street the meseta stretches out as far as the eye can see. Why are they afraid to simply allow the meseta to invade? What is being safeguarded by those few meters of green? This afternoon, from this corner, those fussy gardens look like tiny dogs, barking wildly at a big one, who doesn't even know they exist.

The map is deceptive, making it look like the river can be seen from very nearby Las Heras: the Deseado River, which flows from the Andes and empties into the Atlantic Ocean. But that's not the case; the Deseado cannot be seen because when it gets to Las Heras, it goes underground. You look at the map before traveling there, before arriving at Las Heras, and then you feel like one of those medieval sailors who, when he finally got up the nerve to go beyond where the world map said "terra incognita," found instead a purely aquatic landscape. Maps still carry out their particular form of deceit. In order to reach the river from Las Heras, you have to travel about forty kilometers through terrain that could be dubbed the Love Zone. As we drive, we see one car here, another one over there, all of them functioning as mobile love hotels. They look so small in comparison to the vastness of the landscape, as if they were toy cars and the child who set them up was playing at sexual discovery. When we reach what they point to as the river, I see that it isn't a watercourse but rather a large gash through the meseta, like a wide, deep wound that disrupts everything: what had been flat terrain turns into a kind of cliff. From up here, for the first time in my life, I see an underground river; I see the route but not the water and, in some sections where I assume the groundwater is closer to the surface, tiny bits of precarious vegetation appear. It reminds me of those dolls with heads made of well-fertilized dirt and seeded with miniature grass, which could end up looking like hair if you had the will to believe and the constancy to water them regularly.

This phenomenon of a river going underground, which is not at all common, also occurs in Salta, at the point where the Calchaquí River runs through San Carlos, and local legend attributes it to a curse. Apparently, they say, San Carlos was a prosperous and peaceful town until one morning the parish priest discovered that the church's best chalice, covered in gold and rubies, had disappeared. The authorities spent days and nights looking for it but found nothing. The deputy mayor even dared to conduct searches of the most respectable houses. Nothing. The priest then played his last card: if the chalice did not appear within three Sundays, he said, a curse would be visited upon the person who possessed it. The mestizo de rigueur who'd stolen it panicked, it seems, when he heard, and decided to bury it along the riverbank so that nobody would find it. When the third Sunday arrived and the chalice was still hidden there, the curse fell upon the river and it began to flow underground.

> The curse turned what had been a smiling, happy valley into a place of misfortune and sorrow. Today, only a wisp of memory remains of its mansions and splendor . . . The outlook for the town of San Carlos is only ruin and devastation. The first impression it gives is of

depression and distress, and to live there seems like a punishment. What for us would be cause for despair, leads to apathetic resignation in the inhabitants of San Carlos. For in the air can still be heard the angry voice casting its evil curse. And, under that curse, the river-bed creaks, the rocks knock against each other like mad prisoners, and a clear sound, like metal being deposited on the rocks, cries piteously throughout the afternoons and nights, filling the air with anguish and terror.

Calchiquíe Superstitions, Pablo Fortuny

That's why Juancho left Las Heras, and now he's here only for a visit. Who wants to stay in a place where nothing or only horrible things ever happen? His friends who stayed here would also leave if they could, but it's not easy to leave Las Heras. He never even had to think about it. He was simply born with the idea of getting out of here. Like a reflex. As if it were congenital. When he was in primary school, he'd ditch class and go to the service station at the entrance to town to see if anybody with plates from other places drove by. He'd sit on the curb in front of the tire shop and wait for them. Sometimes not a single one would stop. The main road comes from the east, from the sea, and traverses the territory from one side to the other, all the way to the mountains, but there is a bend at Las Heras so that the road bypasses the town. It's a little bend but significant enough to make it so that nobody feels obliged to stop here. People usually fill up with gas in Truncado then drive right past, straight to the mountains, or vice versa. That little bend in the road wasn't on his, Ramiro's, side, but still he'd go back to the service station every chance he got. He'd sit there and wait. Sometimes the guys at the tire shop would tease him, ask if he'd lost his girlfriend. He wouldn't bother to respond. He had to remain vigilant. A car might drive by, and he knew he wouldn't have a moment to lose. He had to move quickly, find out where the plates were from, go up as close as possible to see what life was like inside that car, and be capable of intercepting whoever got out to ask them something. Sometimes he managed to carry out all those steps; other times he had to settle for some of them. If he had to choose, he'd skip the part of looking in the car. He'd look at the plates and then he'd approach whoever got out, usually the man who was driving. He'd ask him where he was going, where he was coming from. Anything, the first thing that came out. He liked it best when the plates were from Buenos Aires; people from there, *porteños*, were his favorite prey. He'd ask them questions just to hear them talk, that's all, with that typical, lovely accent. Now that he lives in Buenos Aires he's pretty much gotten used to it. To listen to, though not to speak. A lot of people still ask him if he's from the interior. Sometimes, so they'd talk to him longer, he'd offer to wash their windshield, buy them a cola at the shop. That's how he'd keep them there a little longer. That's how he learned about a lot of things: how many were in the family, how what they'd seen on this trip to the South compared to where they lived. That's how he assembled his ideas about the whole country. He didn't let truck drivers participate in his plan because they're liars. They spend a lot of time alone, and this turns people into liars. Must be because they make up characters to keep them company, and then they talk without being able to distinguish very well between themselves and real people. He really doesn't know why they're like that, to tell the truth, but he knows they are. He needed concrete facts, not any old thing they wanted to throw at him. In fact, he always knew that he was going to leave, but what he didn't know was where he was going to go. Buenos Aires always attracted him because of those wide avenues, the noise, the discos, and the soccer stadium, La Bombonera. But that's not the only reason he chose it. Not because of his mother's insistence, either; she's always supported him in everything and especially his desire to leave. She, like his friends, would have liked to leave, too. But it's not easy to leave Las Heras. What clinched it for him was a girl, one of those girls who stopped on the road. She was in a red car, a Chevy. She was riding in the back seat alone, an only child. He can still remember that day, the sky was totally overcast. Her parents got out and a while later, so did she, with a sleepy face. As soon as she got out of the car, she stepped into a puddle of oil in the station. She looked at the puddle, lifted her eyes, saw that he was looking at her, and smiled at him as if they were school friends caught smoking in the bathroom. Her charm and their complicity totally enchanted him. He thought that if that had happened to a girl from here, to any of the girls who on Friday afternoons saunter along the main street, she would have rushed to see if she could wipe the oil off her shoe on the ground, and she would have made one of those nothing-to-see-here faces. But she didn't; she looked at him and smiled, and he thought that all the girls in Buenos Aires would be like her. Now he knows they're not, but now he's there. Luckily, because it's not easy to leave Las Heras.

After 1997, the community and institutions in Las Heras began to get organized, seeking options for dealing with the crisis, aware that this was not a transitory problem, as at other times, but something more permanent. Apathy and malaise had become a generalized attitude, mostly in the young people, who saw their lives as lacking horizons.

Socioeconomic analysis cited above

How can one reconcile this lack of horizon cited in the report, I wonder, with the limitless horizons constantly mentioned in Patagonian travel brochures?

• • •

The teachers were always very kind to Romina: they let her bring her little brothers to class and everything. Both of them, the seven-year-old and the nine-year-old. That's how old they are now, but when she used to bring them to school the oldest was five. They behaved themselves perfectly. They'd save a couple of desks in the back against the wall for them, and she'd sit them down there as soon as she arrived. They'd stay there quietly, mostly without making a peep. She would watch them out of the corner of her eye. That worked out well but it didn't last long, to tell the truth. After a while, which luckily sometimes coincided with recess, they'd get bored and start making noise, and she'd have to take them outside. If it was hot, she'd take them to the yard, but anyway, it's never really hot here. Sometimes a friend would watch them. Depends: at first, when the teachers first gave her permission to bring them, a bunch of her friends would help. The bell would ring, and there'd be like ten of them who'd take them out to recess, all of them running around and playing with the little ones. They'd drag them from one place to another. It was a party. A lot more fun than thinking about some mathematical theorem, or the subject and the predicate. Sometimes even some of the guys would offer to take them out for a walk, imagine that. But that didn't last long; within a month, at most, her friends got interested in other things. So-and-so got it on with so-and-so; I haven't gotten mine in two or three months; she swore to me; et cetera. Romina would come with her little brothers, sit them down at the desks in the back, take them out at recess, but soon, only if she was lucky would her friends give them a supposedly affectionate pat on the head, and then they'd continue on their way. One day one of her brothers fell on the cement in the yard and split open his head, and to get someone to help her she had to shout at them not to be such slobs, to do something, call somebody. They were leaning against the wall, she remembers, and they just stared at her. They looked like sacks of potatoes propped up against the wall of a shed. But now, now that she's twenty-one, she's used to all that. Used to them really leaving her alone with the kids. The teachers no, never. They let her bring them, gave them crackers, asked after their health, made sure they were eating well. Thanks to them, she could finish school. Even the last grade, and she never had to retake an exam. When they'd get back from school, she'd sit her brothers down again in front of the TV and do her homework. Honestly, the boys are a couple of saints. They even call her mamá. At first, truth is, she didn't like that. She still remembers what happened. Romina was in the laundry room, separating out the dirtiest clothes from the ones that only needed to be washed once, when the older one, the one who's nine now, called her mamá for the first time. It had already been about a year or more since their mother had left and left her, their older sister, to take care of them, but the boys were always capable of recognizing that, the difference between the two: between Romina, the older sister, and the mother. She wasn't actually the oldest, because there was Eva, who was older than her, but Eva had left home when she was fifteen, when her mother first started going out with Esteban, the father of the boys, her little brothers, but not of her and Eva. But her little brothers had never even seen Eva, not even once, because she left that day and never showed up again, neither hide nor hair. She didn't even write to her, not ever, even though they'd gotten along so well when they were little. Nothing, so Romina ended up as the boys' oldest sister. Until that day in the laundry room. The wind was terribly strong, she remembers, because when she heard that "mamá" she thought she'd heard wrong because of how much noise the wind was making. She'd left the boys with the TV on and gone to do the laundry. Esteban brings her his dirty clothes twice a week, and those are the two days she has the most work at home, the other days are easier. It was one of those days when the clothes were awful. There are times when the oil wells explode and things get really ugly: nothing can remove those huge grease stains. But worse than the grease is the dirt, the dust, the usual stuff. All the same, she's very organized: two days she washes, and two she irons. She prefers the ironing: she puts on music or watches TV with the boys. She can't do that with the noise of the washing machine. That day there were two things making noise, come to think of it: the wind and the washing machine. But she heard it right. Martincito, the older one, was standing in the doorway of the laundry room and said mamá. Some sentence before that, a question she'll never know what, and at the end, mamá, very clearly. She turned around and slapped him so hard his nose started to bleed. It was a real mess: her brother's shouts, the washing machine, the clothes tossed around, the blood gushing out of him. More clothes to wash, she thought. The clothes of that nutcase and now of this punk, there'll never be an end to it. Never. That night when Esteban arrived, dinner wasn't ready or anything. She threw together whatever she could and during dinner she didn't look up from her plate. Esteban, who sometimes complains that when he arrives, exhausted, she makes his head spin with all her chatter and storytelling, he didn't understand. It's not that she tells him anything in particular, but she spends the whole day alone with the boys and honestly she needs to talk to somebody. She doesn't have any girlfriends, because the girls are into other things, or they're so busy with their own kids that they don't have time to visit her. That day, she couldn't say anything. Nor did she want to tell him because she knew how difficult it had been for Esteban when her mother left him for somebody else, and then for another and another. So why would she talk to him about her mother, remind him of her. Poor Esteban, he'd also been good to her. Like the teachers. He let her stay at the house, and he works so that they all have food to eat. She takes care of the boys, but he's definitely the one that allows it; if it weren't for him, she wouldn't have a pot to piss in. Her mother left all three guys, and her, too. She lives somewhere around there, but she never shows up. Better that way. Romina doesn't want to see her ever again in her life. Not see her or hear anything

about her. That's why that day it was so hard on her, that anyone, especially her little brother, would confuse her with her
mother, a person capable of abandoning them. She'd already
had to deal with that with her father, but it's more understandable with a father. With some fathers, to tell the truth, because
she thinks about Esteban and realizes that he would never do
something like that. Never. Esteban works fifteen-hour shifts
out there, at the wells, and all of it just to feed them. How can
someone abandon a person like that? After a while she was
able to talk about it, thanks to them renting the room in the
back to Giménez. He's somebody she can tell everything to, he
listens to her with an incredible amount of patience. Giménez
lives out in the country, but he has to come to Las Heras constantly to buy tools, buy something, get payment for something
else. The thing is, he comes two or three times a month. Lately
he comes more often. She's happy. She bakes him a cake and
leaves it on the table, sometimes it's even still warm when he
arrives. The last time, she used a new recipe she found in a
magazine, one of those special days when she decides that she
deserves a visit to the hairdresser. A cake with nuts and dulce
de leche. Giménez was so happy. She made maté, called him,
and they spent a couple of hours talking, eating cake. Like always. Honestly, ever since he showed up she feels more relaxed. And Esteban does, too, she thinks. Now she talks to him
only about what's necessary, none of this telling him about the
last telenovela she saw that afternoon. Everything's more bal-
anced, you could say. Because, on the other hand, with Esteban, as she just told me, she doesn't talk about everything. She
can't tell him about her mother or the sorrow she wakes up
with some mornings. On top of him feeding her and letting her

stay at the house, she can't go around talking to him about those things. But with Giménez it's different; she even feels like she's the homeowner because he pays her directly. Even though Romina then gives it to Esteban, she's the one who opens her hand to take the money, she's the one who's always at home. And Giménez seems to realize that, based on how respectfully he treats her. And to think she tells him everything, everything. He might feel bad because of certain things, might hate her and not talk to her anymore because of others. Like the slap she gave Martincito, for example. He could say she's a bad, heartless person. But he doesn't; Giménez listens to her and looks down, as if he were watching the river flow by. He barely speaks, just here and there. He's never given her nasty looks or anything. Fact is, it's even better than having a girlfriend, because girlfriends, you know how they are: today they're here and tomorrow their attention is focused on whatever else.

• • •

During the last decade of the twentieth century, oil production in Las Heras increased significantly, and in 1994, Los Perales—the neighboring oil field to the northeast, where most of the town's residents work—became, for Repsol-YPF, the second largest oil-producing region in the country. Whereas other oil towns were abandoned and dismantled during that decade, Las Heras saw its population double. But neither these figures nor those of the industry's balance sheets seem to have touched the town, which continues to view oil as a resource that condemns rather than saves, and that, moreover, others always take. Las Heras seems to embody, like no other place in the

South, all the speeches, from Pigafetta onward, that defined Patagonia as a place akin to the netherworld.

• • •

Say what they will, it's all seven of them. Say what they will. What happened is that with her, they met their match. They were able to do it to the others, to the poor family men who now wander around like lost souls, like vagabonds; to those people who had their heads in their account books, their children's school, should they build a house, buy a new car, and suddenly all they had were stories and more stories. You've got to know, you've got to be able to imagine what it feels like when your own mind gets taken over by the seeds of destruction, you have to feel what it's like when the enemy is inside you, right there inside you. They also did it to the teenagers, to those little minds that are preoccupied with the latest boyfriend or girlfriend, with getting whatever substance they want to consume. They take away their alpha, that's what they do. The stories take away their alpha and that's how they destroy them. But they met their match with her, because she has the power to confront them. And they won't ever beat her. She's not ever going to become a bum or commit suicide. Why? Because she has powers, she's telepathic. And that's why she can expose them, question them, upset them, resist them. Because she's telepathic, and that's why she doesn't succumb like the rest of them, who simply listen to the stories. She has the power to expose them.

And that's why, one night, another of those tormented nights, a night when she'd carried her powers to the extreme, she finally got the answer. She confronted them, she questioned them in the middle of their stories, and that's how she found out. She discovered the people who are the source of these practices, the storytellers who are looking for the winning number. So, right then, with all the energy that the gods have given her, she said: Who is looking?! Who?! And that's when she got the answer, that's when she found out, after nights and nights of insomnia that led others to their destruction and her to the truth; that's when she found out it was them, the owners of the Lottery House. And this was thanks to her being telepathic. She's not a seer, like they go around saying here, like the newspaper from Comodoro says. And it's not true, like the newspaper said, that she threatened that kid, who's the devil incarnate. It's all lies. But they're going to have to deal with her, she's going to report them, and they're going to have to sell everything they've stolen in order to pay her. In that newspaper article, the lottery agent, the head of that sect, said that the walls of his son-in-law's house were smeared with paint twice, and he also said that she'd gone to the school of that little devil they spawned to tell them not to let him enter, how he was harmful to the environment. All lies! What a trial they'll have to go through! She doesn't go around threatening folks, they invent those things. One of these days, she'll go and straight out: Bam! She'll shoot them and their mothers down. Period. She's not somebody who goes around threatening folks.

The scenes are highlights from Pirate's career as a fantasist-surrogate, and go back to when he was carrying, everywhere he went, the mark of Youthful Folly

growing in an unmistakable Mongoloid point, right out
of the middle of his head. He had known for a while
that certain episodes he dreamed could not be his own.
This wasn't through any rigorous daytime analysis of
content, but just because he *knew*. But then came the
day when he met, for the first time, the real owner of a
dream he, Pirate, had had: . . .

from Gravity's Rainbow *by Thomas Pynchon*

Sandra offers me a cup of tea, thinking, perhaps, that it's a
way of calming down, because every time she remembers what
the newspapers said, her permanent state of irritation rises one
pitch higher. Or perhaps, in her bizarre version of hospitality, tea gets offered to the visitor after at least three hours of
conversation rather than in the initial few minutes. Or perhaps she thinks it's another way to warm us up, to keep the
kitchen warm. Sandra has all the burners on as well as the
oven door open. One of her dogs—one of the seven stray dogs
she's brought in from the street, surely the one most sensitive
to the cold—has taken extreme measures: it has jumped onto
the open oven door and stares at us from there, happy on its
heated porch, all white against the background of the black
oven. The other dogs circulate around the kitchen, though also
not in the usual places; they walk across the counter and over
the table where we are drinking tea. They do it so naturally
that they seem to place the laws of gravity in doubt, and what
do they care about the rules of civility. For moments at a time,
I continue to listen to her even though I stop seeing her: Sandra's face disappears behind the silhouette of a dog walking

down the length of the table. If they knew what the poor things suffered when they took her there, to the asylum in Gallegos, she tells me. They are the only ones who don't point fingers at her. They and the people of YPF, who are so kind, who kept her job for her and offered her help because they don't buy into those ridiculous stories the people around here like to tell. That comment coincides with the passage of a black dog with a long body and short legs; when Sandra's face reappears, I think I see some signs of mild relaxation, a small crack through which something akin to serenity could filter, but it doesn't last long. Her facial muscles quickly contract, as if she were a hunting dog herself. All the blinds in her house are drawn, and the armchairs are covered with thick plastic sheeting that is covered in dirt, as if she'd just returned after a long journey. When the dogs aren't walking across the table, they're on the armchairs. There's one for each of them.

She has lots of proof, written proof of corruption. Proof that shows that those people at the Lottery House are tricking people to get the numbers, proof that shows that they pay the press to distort the truth. Proof that shows that they spend their time focusing their attention, night and day, on destroying the minds of the Lashereños. She has the proof, she says, and she's going to show it to me. She disappears from the kitchen. All the dogs follow her except one, the one who's inside the oven. I get up from my chair to check if he's alive. I'm careful to avoid a bunch of cardboard boxes that Sandra has piled in a corner of the kitchen, on which, high up, is some kind of lantern into which flows an infinite number of cables of various widths and colors. The tea Sandra made is very strong and leaves my tongue feeling rough, like a cat's. There's no noise in the house.

Sandra returns a short time later with a stack of papers. All the proof, she says. She's going to go through them one by one to show me, she promises. First she pulls out an article from the *Crónica* newspaper from Comodoro, which she already told me about, the one that irritates her most, from March 2002.

42   **Crónica**   Sábado 16 de marzo de 2002

Presunto caso paranormal en Las Heras

Una vidente denunció a un agenciero de 'meterse en sus sueños'

La mujer dice que es para sacarle los números de quiniela

«La intromisión en los sueños es contínua», dice la denunciante

«Tuve que denunciarla porque empezó ameterse con la familia» dijo el agenciero

«Siempre jugaba, pero nunca acertó»

Lo dijo una senadora: «Esta mujer dijo que los iba a matar a todos»

A psychic accuses lottery agent of "invading her dreams." The woman says it is to get the winning lottery numbers from her. "Their intrusion into dreams is constant," says the accuser. "I had to report her because she started to harass my family," said the agent. A senator told her: "This woman said she was going to kill all of them."

Proof that they pay the newspapers, Sandra tells me, from the fact that, next to the sentence, "Their intrusion into dreams is constant," there appears another, a quote from the lottery agent: "I had to report her because she started to harass my family." I tell her that it's a basic rule of journalism to give both sides, and I manage to irritate her more than the article does. Do I or don't I want to see everything that's in these folders? Do I or don't I trust her? If I keep on like this she's going to kick me out of the house like she already kicked out so many good-for-nothings who've come to interview her. I'll go flying over to the other side of the street. One of the dogs steps on the folder, forcing Sandra to tug on it so she can take more papers out. I keep drinking the tea that now, in addition to being harsh, is cold. She takes out the second document, and I see that it's a photocopy of the same article. I look at her, I look at the dog who looks at us from the oven, I remain silent. They're all incriminated, she tells me. She's going to report all of them: the lottery agent, the chief of police, the judge in Pico Truncado, everybody. She pulls out a third document: the same article. They're going to have to dig money up out of the ground to pay for the settlement she's going to win, she tells me. She might not have ever won anything in the lottery, but now she's going to be rich, a millionaire, once they pay her for what they did to her. She takes out a fourth document, and I realize that it is the same article, photocopied to death.

More and more copies of the same thing. It reminds me of that scene in *The Shining* where Jack Nicholson's wife finally manages to see what her husband has been writing since they came to that empty and isolated hotel in the mountains as winter caretakers. She knows that he's working on his new book because the whole time, echoing through the endless corridors of that empty hotel, the dull banging on the keys of his typewriter can be heard. Until finally one day she manages to distract him in another wing of the hotel and goes to look at the papers on his desk, piled up next to the typewriter. She picks them up, and instead of a plot with characters and dialogues and description and experimentation, she finds the same sentence repeated ad infinitum: "All work and no play makes Jack a dull boy."

"Their intrusion into dreams is constant." "I had to report her because she began to harass my family." "All work and no play makes Jack a dull boy." "Their intrusion into dreams is constant." "I had to report her because she began to harass my family." "All work and no play makes Jack a dull boy." "Their intrusion into dreams is constant." "I had to report her because she began to harass my family." "All work and no play makes Jack a dull boy." "Their intrusion into dreams is constant." "I had to report her because she began to harass my family." "All work and no play makes Jack a dull boy." "Their intrusion into dreams is constant." "I had to report her because she began to harass my family." "All work and no play makes Jack a dull boy." "Their intrusion into dreams is constant." "I had to report her because she began to harass my family." "All work and no play makes Jack a dull boy." "Their intrusion into dreams is constant." "I had to report her because she began to harass my family." "Their intrusion into dreams is constant." After I finish my last sip of tea, I see Sandra get up from the table and throw out the tea she poured into her own cup without even tasting it. There is a large aluminum pot over one of the lit burners. This whole subject is very complex, it's really only for those who understand these things. Considering that I don't even know what it is to enter an alpha state, I shouldn't ask any questions, she tells me, and she looks to see that the water is at a rolling boil. She pushes through the steam with a large fork, like a trident, and stabs it into a piece of meat that she then lifts, with triumph, like a quarry. She is so skinny and bony that I don't know how she manages to lift that piece of flesh that fate should one day return to her own scrawny body. I shouldn't, she repeats to me, and smells it. The seven dogs dance around her.

• • •

This telepathy business hasn't always been like this, she tells me, this access she has to those voices that isn't available to all mortals. Many years ago, the voices spoke to her only when she summoned them, and they were even charming, she says, they could even be considered affectionate. They would whisper to her a fact, some suggestion or other. She also talked back to them. Not like now, when she wakes up in the middle of the night screaming at them, scolding them. She used to talk politely to them, gently. In other words, they carried on a dialogue.

There was even a time when the voices were her allies. And she never took advantage of that. When she played the lottery, for example. She always played, that's why she knows so well the people who now want to destroy her. But she never took advantage of her telepathic powers to win. That also came out in the newspaper, that old man saying that she always played but never won. Of course she never won, because she never wanted to take advantage of her gifts. She wanted to win like any other mortal. The voices, the knowledge and information the voices told her, she had to use them for more altruistic purposes. They helped her to survive, to tell the truth, to do something much more interesting than what she does now, taking care of the gardens of Repsol executives. The voices would give her information, reveal things to her that nobody knew; they were the tools of her trade. Information about people who disappeared, mostly. The police looked for those people, so they were willing to pay her for the information.

Around here, people disappear a lot. One day they leave their house, and they never come back. For no reason, with no warning. One day, they simply never show up again. Who knows what drop overflows what glass. Or not even; maybe it's nothing like that. One morning, they simply get dressed a little more warmly (as if deep down they had an intuition) and start walking. They're going, they think they're going, somewhere: to buy fruit, to the post office, to a friend's place. On one block, at some street corner, they see as always the same billboard advertising cold drinks, with rusty edges, bright paint over rusty metal, and that image they've seen so many times falls apart. They see it as if for the first time, but not because of the curiosity or excitement you get when you see something for the first time, but because of despair, a lack of references. They're not fed up with anyone, and there's not anything they want to run away from; that image simply informs them that nothing will ever be the same again. The known has been swept away, out from under their feet. There's nowhere to go back to, so they don't. They leave, disappear.

The voices used to tell Sandra about those people. They would tell her where they were, but not only that. They would tell her where their minds were, what was going on in their heads. It was lovely: like sitting in a movie theater and seeing a mind on the big screen. Random images appeared to her, or a whole story told in a certain way and, a while later, in a totally different way. Even with different characters added in. Or with secondary characters who turned into main characters a while later. It's incredible how interesting others' minds are if you have the time to devote to them. She'd settle in there, but sanely, that is, discreetly. Sometimes, when she'd see from those images that the best thing for that person would be to continue along the path that he had finally taken that morning—to disappear, look for other points of references, other kinds of support—when she'd see that from her seat, Sandra would simply keep quiet. It was hard for her that the police thought she was good but not that good because there were some cases she didn't manage to solve. But she didn't care: she knew that sometimes it was best to keep quiet. She knew that she was doing the right thing. But those were other times, and now there's nothing. Now it's impossible to distinguish what's right from what's wrong with those voices that are trying to take over her head.

Once, just to give one example, she solved the disappearance of a baby. It's incredible, we think a baby hasn't got anything in its head, but that's not true. It has millions of things, and not only impressions, also memories. Memories of its own from inside the belly, from its birth, but also memories of those who came before. As if minds in that state were a catalyst for the most recent past. This baby had disappeared along with its mother, but the one she managed to find, the one who spoke to her in his own voice, was the baby, not the mother. When the police found him, he was already dead. Sometimes it turned out that she would find them when they were still alive, and others they found when they were already dead. That's how life is. And death, too, of course. Unpredictable. That baby had drowned in the bathroom in the cemetery, its white head stuffed into the toilet. Who, in whose head can such a thing fit? In some mothers' heads, so it seems.

Her own children should think about those cases now that they don't want to talk to her anymore. About how there are truly cold-hearted mothers, not like her. But they decided not to talk to her anymore. Both of them, her son and her daughter. They both live here, in Las Heras, a few blocks from her house, and they don't even want to talk to her. So it goes. Biting the hand that feeds you. Then they tell you about how girls are more attached to their mothers. They both conspired with that other one, that monster her sister. Her own sister, Sandra's. And they say that siblings stick together. She's the one who put her into that insane asylum in Río Gallegos. Her sister, who goes around giving grandiose speeches in Perito Moreno, where she lives. She works for the Ministry of Culture, a director or something like that. Recently she organized for schoolchildren a show of painters who didn't have hands, from somewhere else, I think from Córdoba. A whole big to-do: she was in charge of gathering together school-age kids to show them that the paths to art are unfathomable, that when someone is talented and dedicated, no obstacle can prevent that someone from embracing art. The show, it seems, would teach an important lesson. She gathered together the children to wait for the bus that was coming from far-away Córdoba, a whole big to-do. Everybody eagerly waiting there, and what does her sister see when the invited artists start to get off the bus? That they have hands. They have stubs, or whatever, but hands after all. And she was horrified, totally disappointed. Like anybody would be, she complained, and she ranted and raved against people who don't use language with precision. No hands? Ha! A whole lesson ruined, she said, and how hard it is here for teenagers to get any—any at all! as usual, she underlines her words with her red painted fingernail—proof that things can be achieved in spite of great difficulties. Can I believe such a scoundrel could be her sister? A person who is capable of that, of thinking that was a trick, she's the same one who put Sandra into an asylum. It was after she filed the complaint against the owners of the Lottery House. As soon as she published that letter in the local newspaper, her sister started to set the traps to have her put away. That's why she did it: her sister, like so many other human beings, is not ready to deal with very much reality.

Sandra looks at the city with a confused expression on her face, a mixture of desperation in the face of others' indifference and pride at having arrived at the correct hypothesis. Last night they came, she saw them in her dreams, all of them on a balcony, focused. Swollen, blue, as if under the effects of a recent death. Day and night they focus, perform evil deeds. They bring all the evil to this town. Day and night. Day and night. While people are trying to lead a regular life, a normal life, they concentrate on taking over their lives. With her, with Sandra, they can't do it, it's not so easy. That's what they're finding out. They leave her in a daze, they invade her head, but they can't crush her. Those seven don't crush her and neither does the psychiatrist conniving with her whole family or the lawyer or the entire Supreme Court. Nothing she had to see or deal with when they took her there, to Gallegos, has crushed her. They put her away in the asylum in Gallegos and they tried to control her with pills. They'd put five pills in her hand, as if she were a pigeon in the plaza, frantic for a piece of popcorn. It's not so easy, as they're now finding out. She'd make a face, as if she were resigned, then she'd flush them down the toilet. It's not so easy. There went the little pills, their beautiful bright colors spinning around in the swirling water. The things she had to see and hear there, the way they treat people. Everybody was desperate. They say they let her out because the term during which the institution can keep a mentally ill patient was over, that's what they call those poor people. But she knows they let her out so that she wouldn't keep being a witness, finding things out. All the people around her, they're the ones who are mentally ill. But it's not going to be so easy. She's going to denounce all of them, they're going to end up paying her money they don't have. All of them. They're going to be ruined. She's on to this whole web of voices that inhabit her, on to them and everybody who's behind them. She knows how far the conspiracy goes, she knows it has international connections. This is no game. This isn't for beginners. She is the last bastion. The town doesn't realize it, but Sandra is watching over them. Protecting them, their protective wall.

Night and day. Night and day.

MARÍA SONIA CRISTOFF (Trelew, Patagonia, 1965) is the author of five works of fiction and nonfiction, including *False Calm* and *Include Me Out*, and lives in Buenos Aires, where she teaches creative writing. Her journalism can be found in *Neue Zürcher Zeitung*, *Perfil*, and *La Nación*. She has edited volumes on literary nonfiction (*Idea crónica* and *Pasaje a Oriente*) and participated in a series of collective works. Her work has been translated into six languages. This is her first book to appear in English.

KATHERINE SILVER is an award-winning literary translator and the former director of the Banff International Literary Translation Centre. Her most recent and forthcoming translations include works by Daniel Sada, César Aira, Horacio Castellanos Moya, Julio Cortázar, Juan Carlos Onetti, and Julio Ramón Ribeyro.

Transit Books is a nonprofit publisher of international and American literature, based in Oakland, California. Founded in 2015, Transit Books is committed to the discovery and promotion of enduring works that carry readers across borders and communities. Visit us online to learn more about our forthcoming titles, events, and opportunities to support our mission.

TRANSITBOOKS.ORG